Assertion Training Workshop

Leader Guide

Revised Edition

Laura G. Manis

LP **LEARNING PUBLICATIONS, INC.**
Holmes Beach, Florida

ISBN 1-55691-140-8

© 1985, 1998 by Laura G. Manis

All rights reserved. No part of this book may be reproduced or transmitted in any form or by any means, electronic or mechanical, including photocopying and recording, or by any information or retrieval systems, without permission in writing from the publisher.

Learning Publications, Inc.
5351 Gulf Drive
P.O. Box 1338
Holmes Beach, FL 34218-1338

Printing: 5 4 3 2 1   Year: 2 1 0 9 8

Printed in the United States of America.

Contents

Preface vii
Introduction xi

Session 1: Learning How to Identify Assertive Behavior

Overview 1
Workshop Overview 2
Mini-Lecture: What is Assertion Training? 3
Training Steps 4
Exercise: Introductions 6
Discussion: Workshop Expectations and Procedures 7
Exercise: Ice-Breaker — Do You Like Artichokes? 9
Exercise: I Need to Think About That 10
Discussion: Behaviors Defined and Explored 11
Exercise: Discrimination 17
Exercise: Subjective Unit of Disturbance Scale (SUDS Score) 20
Exercise: Body Language 22
Exercise: Absurd Topics 23
Exercise: Desensitization to Eye Contact 24
Beginning and Ending the Session 25
Exercise: The Link 25
Homework 26
Homework Readings: Is Being Assertive Being Selfish? 27
Homework Activity: Discrimination Test 28
Key for Discrimination Test 30
Homework Activity: Sample Daily Log of Assertive Behavior 31

Session 2: Respecting Rights

Overview 33
Homework Review 34
Exercise: Making Positive Self-Statements 35
Mini-Lecture: Rights and Responsibilities 36
Discussion: Personal Rights 37
Exercise: Others Rights 39
Exercise: Rights Auction 40
Rights Auction (Securities) — Are You Willing to Give These Up? 41
Exercise: Rights Role Play 42
Role Playing Rehearsal (RPR) Observer's Checklist 44
Closing the Session 45

Homework 45
Homework Reading: Irrational Beliefs 46
Homework Activity: Exercises in Concreteness 49

Session 3: Blocks to Assertion

Overview 53
Homework Review 54
Mini-Lecture: Blocks to Assertion 54
Exercise: Relaxation to Relieve Stress 56
Exercise: Rational-Emotive Imagery 59
Exercise: Stop! 60
Closing the Session 61
Homework 61
Homework Reading: Dealing with Disapproval 62
Homework Activity: Developing Self-Statements for Coping with Anger 63
Homework Activity: Developing Self-Statements for Coping with Stress 64

Session 4: Refusing Requests

Overview 65
Homework Review 66
Exercise: Giving Compliments 66
Exercise: Persistence — The Broken Record Technique 68
Exercise: Combining Persistence with Empathy 71
Combining Persistence with Empathy 73
Closing the Session 75
Homework 75
Homework Reading: Helpful Hints for Saying "No" to Unfair Requests and Demands 75

Session 5: Expressing Feelings

Overview 77
Homework Review 78
Exercise: Admitting Mistakes 78
Exercise: Criticism (Negative Inquiry) 79
Exercise: Expressing Feelings Assertively 81
"I" Language Assertion 82
Exercise: Desensitization to Criticism 84
Closing the Session 87
Homework 87
Homework Reading: Dealing with Criticism or Anger 87
Summary 88

Homework Reading: Negative Feedback to Others 88
Homework Reading: Disagreeing 89
Homework Activity: "I Want" List 89

Session 6: Personal Situations

Overview 91
Homework Review 92
Exercise: Breaking into Conversations 92
Exercise: Behavior Rehearsal and Escalation 93
Exercise: Post-Session Self-Assessment 95
Closing the Session and Ending the Workshop 97
Exercise: Strength Bombardment 97
Homework 98
Homework Reading: Step by Step to Responsible Assertion 98
Homework Activity: Goal Setting 99

Appendix A: Self-Assessment 101
Appendix B: Daily Log of Assertive Behavior 103
Appendix C: Screening Protocol for Assertion Training 105
Appendix D: Principles of Ethical Practice of Assertive Behavior Training 107
Appendix E: Suggested Agenda for a One-Day Workshop 115
Appendix F: Advanced Assertion Training 117
Appendix G: Glossary..119
Appendix H: What Do You Say? 121
Appendix I: Bibliography 123

Preface

Assertion Training Workshop will serve as a guide to mental health professionals, business managers, human development specialists and educators wishing to do ongoing assertion training. The material included is sufficient for a beginning six-session workshop. This model has been used numerous times; the feedback and evaluations indicate that it has been very successful. Assertion Training Workshop is appropriate for use with a variety of populations including students, women's groups, hospital and business personnel, and the general population. The *Assertion Training Workshop* design also lends itself to a variety of settings and is appropriate for use in schools, community centers, churches, continuing education programs, and conference settings.

While preparing to write a revised manual I realized that I could not improve very much on the old manual despite the fact of a sea of change in the number of women in the work force and in supervisory positions. However, I have noticed some changes in behavior in recent workshops. More women are using aggressive behavior in the belief that they are being assertive and more men are using passive-aggressive behavior. As roles change, we must be careful about assuming the worst behavior of the opposite gender.

Because of societal changes, in this edition you will find more attention paid to workplace situations.

By and large though, most people have the same problems.

Acknowledgments

I would like to thank several people who helped improve the content and format of the manual. Kari Lockwood, Merry Pattison, June Mochizuki, and Sanny Nutter contributed suggestions and field tested the material. Their stimulating discussion led to greater clarity and insight.

I would also like to express thanks to Odessa Straw, Sue Esman, and Betty Roberts for their assistance in typing many versions of the original manuscript.

Tomara Kafka of Learning Publications brought a clear eye and skill to straighten out muddled language and outdated examples to this edition.

About the Author

Laura G. Manis has spent three decades in counseling and personnel work. She has a special interest in developing programs which meet the unique needs of women. She helped to plan and establish the Center for Women's Services and the Women's Studies Program at Western Michigan University.

Ms. Manis has developed a number of programs for women: SEARCH, to help mature women reassess goals; CONTACT, to help separated and divorced persons readjust; and two programs for school-age women to explore roles, plan ahead, and learn skills for effective living.

Lately Ms. Manis has devoted her energies to working with caregivers of Alzheimer's patients and other long-term care families. She has trained support group facilitators, written a trainer's manual for the same group and organized a grass-roots coalition to work with the Hawaii State Legislature to develop a financing program to help families pay for long-term care.

Ms. Manis is the author of *Womanpower* (Carroll Press), a book which evolved from her work with young women. *Assertion Training Workshop* was developed after eight years of teaching assertion skills to a variety of populations and training large numbers of assertion workshop leaders.

Introduction

Assertion Training Workshop describes a six-session workshop, which meets for two hours once a week. The Leader Guide is divided into six sessions, each session beginning with an outline which includes the goals, materials required, exercises, readings, and homework. A workbook for participants is available. Workbook page numbers and content are indicated in the leader guide.

Many new group members have difficulty thinking of the right words or phrases to use in their assertion exercises. The beginning exercises include practice using suggested wording. As the participants grow in confidence, they will provide their own wording.

The role plays are in sequence from commercial situations to family situations. Expectations of commercial behavior (e.g., with a sales clerk) are generally known and therefore easier for most people. Rules of behavior for social situations are somewhat less rigid, and the concern for its impact on relationships make assertion more difficult. Most difficult of all for many people, are situations involving family members and authority figures. Past history, learned behavior, old feelings, new concerns, and important relationships all have to be considered in changing behavior. In any event, the decision to change any behavior belongs to the participant.

The nine lectures, readings, exercises, and most important, role plays, will provide the participants with conceptual and practical understanding of assertive behavior.

Importance of Role Plays

Role playing fills the gap between reading about behavior change and theory and actually experiencing the behavior and hearing how it effects others.

Role plays are especially important as a means of practicing new behavior in a safe environment and acquiring constructive suggestions on how to improve. Role plays also promote confidence when the actual situation arises and incorporates the behavior into the participant's repertoire of responses so that a more effective response becomes almost automatic.

Some of the distinctive benefits of role plays are:

- It reveals the difference between thinking and doing.
- It makes clear that assertion training is a skill to be learned in the same way riding a bicycle is a skill.
- It shows that the behavior is not only a product of personality but also of the situations in which persons find themselves.
- The use of feedback in role playing trains the participant to be sensitive to the feelings of others and the degree feelings play in determining behavior.
- It helps people to discover their personal faults. For example, using wisecracks or sarcasm often hurts others.
- It permits training in the control of feelings and emotions. For example, repeatedly playing the role of manager gives practice in not becoming annoyed by complaints.

Screening

This guide was developed specifically for a general population, not for those who have serious emotional or psychological problems. For this reason, the use of a screening protocol is recommended; either the one included here (see Appendix C) or one of your own.

Assertion training is not a cure-all. Nor is it intended to help persons in crisis situations, nor is it group psychotherapy. Other populations better served elsewhere include seriously depressed, alcoholic, drug addicted, suicidal, schizophrenic, or hysterical persons. Neither should persons with very low general energy levels be included. Such persons seem to think, feel, and behave minimally. Because of its educational format, there is not enough time to permit in-depth work with any one individual. These persons should be referred to one-to-one counseling or to smaller assertion groups intended for people with special concerns.

The material in this guide has worked well for special populations, such as the blind, the developmentally and physically disable, and persons recovering from mental illness. In these instances, much more time is spent on each exercise, explanations are simplified and repeated, and more time is spent on practice and giving feedback. Only one or two behaviors should be chosen for modification during the six sessions.

Assertion training, as outlined here, is most effective with situationally rather than generally nonassertive persons. Usually situationally nonassertive or situationally aggressive persons are able to begin using assertion techniques quite successfully. However, more caution is required with the generally nonassertive and generally aggressive, and slow and careful practice with another person, preferably a trained therapist or in a special group, is recommended.

Pre- and Post-Assessment

Assessment is an important part of measuring any behavioral changes. A self-assessment instrument which covers the basic skills covered in this manual is located in Appendix A. The pre-session assessment should be completed prior to the first session, either at the time of registration or while waiting for the first session to start. The pre-session assessment can be useful to you in two ways: as a tool for screening and as an aid to you and the participant in identifying the type of behaviors which cause difficulties. (Occasionally, some participants have difficulty thinking of personal situations for role playing. In these instances, they can be referred back to their pre-session self-assessment.)

The post-session assessment is the final activity of the workshop. It provides information about progress made and points out areas in which participants need more practice. An example of a post-assessment instrument is also located in Appendix A. If you prefer assessment instruments that have been validated, I recommend the College Self-Expression Scale* or the Adult Self Expression Scale.**

Principles of Ethical Practice and Training Requirements

It is expected that persons leading groups in assertion training will be professionals meeting the general qualifications as stated in "Principles for Ethical Practice of Assertive Behavior

---
*Galassi, DeLo, Galassi, and Bastien, *Behavior Therapy*, 5, 165-171, 1974.
**Available from Adult Self-Expression Scale, P.O. Box 17174, Charlotte, NC 28211.

Training" (see Appendix D). Minimally, they should prepare themselves by reading the books listed in the reference section and by participating in at least 10 hours of assertive training as a participant and another 10 hours as a facilitator under supervision. Leaders should have previous experience in supervised group work before conducting a group without assistance or supervision. Leaders with little counseling or therapy experience should also have an experienced person available for supervision and consultation.

Assertive behavior training has become popular, and along with this, there is certain evidence of "faddishness." There have been reports of ethically irresponsible practices. For example, there may be leaders who do not adequately differentiate between assertion and aggression. Others may lead participants to expect instant and consistent success and fail to caution or prepare them for the possibility of negative reactions from others.

"Principles for Ethical Practice of Assertive Behavior Training" is the work of professional psychologists and educators and was presented to the American Psychological Association at its national convention in September 1976. I declare support for and adherence to the statement of principles and invite responsible professionals who use these techniques to join me in practicing these principles.

General Training Guidelines

The following is a list of general training strategies that are recommended for incorporation into your assertion training program:

1. Participants who are deficient in assertive behavior will often be hesitant to engage in assertive responses and may become easily discouraged if they are not immediately successful. As a result, it is important for you to provide frequent and sincere verbal praise for initial approximations of assertive behavior by the participants during behavior rehearsal. It is important to increase both the participants' skills and confidence. Emphasize what is positive in their performance.*

2. During behavior rehearsal, praise the participants for what they have done well, then select one or at most two behaviors to improve at any one time.*

3. During early training phases, give concrete feedback to participants by helping them arrive at the exact words and actions they might use in particular situations. A good way to help them start is to ask, "What would you have liked to say?"

4. Video and/or audiotape feedback are quite useful in assertion training programs. Through these media, participants learn to observe and evaluate their own behavior. They also receive constant reinforcement when they view themselves demonstrating appropriate assertive behavior. In addition, you may use video or audiotape to prepare and present short models of assertive interactions to the group.*

5. When working with mixed-gender or mixed-status groups, it is generally helpful to use behavior rehearsal with same-gender or same-status dyad or triads for the first few sessions. Then progress to opposite-gender/mixed-status rehearsals during the later sessions. Most participants find that initially it is less anxiety provoking to learn to assert themselves with

---

*Adapted with permission from Merna Dee Galassi and John P. Galassi, *Assert Yourself: How to Be Your Own Person*, (New York: Human Sciences Press, 1977).

persons of the same sex or status. Thus, beginning with same gender or status groups helps to maintain participants' anxiety at manageable levels.* However, the leader should be watchful for occasions when same gender or same status groups consider their interactions as admissions of "weakness" and do not express themselves sincerely.

6. It is important that participants understand that changes in their behavior may affect their relationships with their families, friends, and associates. Participants who have previously allowed others to make their decisions for them or who have been willing to do almost anything that a spouse or friend demanded, may find that the significant others are not only shocked by their new behavior, but also displeased, at least initially. Therefore, participants should inform significant others in their environments that they are learning to behave assertively and that this may involve changes in their relationships. Participants might be encouraged to ask these persons for feedback and support in their efforts to develop new behaviors.*

7. It is crucial that participants learn to clearly distinguish between nonassertive, aggressive, and assertive behavior. More importantly, they should be able to reflect such discriminations in their own behavior. If assertion training is to be successful, it is extremely important that participants learn assertive, not aggressive, ways of interacting.

8. Participants should rehearse all homework assignments during group sessions before trying them in actual situations.

9. *Assertion Training Workshop* has an educational format. It is not group psychotherapy. If persons are experiencing intense personal anguish or frustration and finding it difficult to hold their lives together, then this group is not the place to begin. This workshop is brief and does not permit much in-depth work with individual participants. As a result, it is likely that their frustration and pain would be heightened, leading to less effective interpersonal behavior. It is recommended that these persons start with one-to-one counseling, and if they desire, that they enroll in an assertiveness workshop later.

10. Participants are free to refuse to participate in any activity. Furthermore, no reasons need be provided for declining to do activities, accept suggestions, or participate in exercises. However, if a group member chooses not to do as suggested by the group leader, he or she is expected to do so in a manner that does not interfere with the choice and participation of other participants.

11. Participants should not rehearse role plays with the same group members each time. By changing partners they will learn how to respond to a variety of personalties.

12. Structure the group procedures so that the participants' involvement is widespread and supportive.

13. Give considerable permission and encouragement for the participants to behave assertively within and outside of the group.

14. Display leadership behavior which is characterized by assertion rather than aggression or nonassertion.

---

*Adapted with permission from Merna Dee Galassi and John P. Galassi, *Assert Yourself: How to Be Your Own Person*, (New York: Human Sciences Press, 1977).

15. Resistance can be handled by asking participants to rehearse their ways of handling a situation, then to practice the assertive way. Encourage them to listen to feedback from other members in their group and then choose whichever method is most satisfying.

Session 1
Learning How to Identify Assertive Behavior

Overview

Goals: To give participants an overview of the workshop; to help participants begin to feel at ease with each other and the structure and methods used; to learn how to distinguish assertive from nonassertive behavior.

Materials: Workbooks, name tags, pencils, newsprint, marking pens

Contents: Pre-Session Self-Assessment (Appendix A – 📖 Workbook p. 4)
Workshop Overview
Mini-Lecture: What is Assertion Training?
Exercise: Introductions
Discussion: Workshop Expectations and Procedures
Exercise: Ice-Breaker: Do You Like Artichokes?
Exercise: I Need to Think About That
Discussion: Behaviors Defined and Explored
Exercise: Discrimination
Exercise: SUDS Scale
Exercise: Body Language
Exercise: Absurd Topics
Exercise: Desensitization to Eye Contact
Beginning and Ending the Session
Exercise: The Line
Homework

📖 Readings: Workshop Expectations and Procedures
Behaviors Defined and Explored
Is Being Assertive Being Selfish?

☑ Activities: Daily Log of Assertive Behavior
Discrimination Test
Introduce Yourself to Three Strangers
Respond: "I need to think about that."

Workshop Overview

(Workbook p. 3)

Session	Main Focus	Exercise	Readings	Homework Other
1	Learning How to Identify Assertive Behavior	Introductions Ice Breaker: Do You Like Artichokes? Discrimination SUDS Scale Body Language Absurd Topic Desensitization to Eye Contact The Link	Workshop Expectations and Procedures Behaviors Defined and Explored Is Being Assertive Being Selfish?	Daily Log of Assertive Behavior Discrimination Test Introduce Yourself to Three Strangers Respond: "I Need to Think About That"
2	Respecting Rights	Making Positive Self-Statements Others' Rights Rights Auction Rights Role Play	Irrational Beliefs	Exercises in Concreteness Uses of Rights Won in Auction Three Positive Self-Statements Daily Log
3	Blocks to Assertion	Owning Rights Relaxation to Relieve Stress Cognitive Restructuring • Rational-Emotive Imagery • STOP! The Link	Dealing with Disapproval	Developing Self-Statements for Coping with Stress Developing Self-Statements for Coping with Anger Practice in Cognitive Restructuring Daily Log
4	Refusing Requests	Giving Compliments Persistence — The Broken Record Technique Combining Persistence with Empathy The Link	Saying "No" to Unfair Requests	Practice Refusing Unreasonable Requests Note Handling of Criticism and Compliments Give Three Compliments Daily Log
5	Expressing Feelings	Admitting Mistakes Criticism (Negative Inquiry) Expressing Feelings Assertively ("I" Language) Desensitization to Criticism (Fogging) The Link	Dealing with Criticism or Anger Negative Feedback to Others Disagreeing	"I-Want" List Daily Log
6	Personal Situations	Breaking into Conversations Behavior Rehearsal and Escalation Strength Bombardment Post-Session Self-Assessment	Step by Step to Responsible Assertion	Goal Setting

2

Session 1

Mini-Lecture: What is Assertion Training?

The following lecture should be given during the first session. Its purpose is to introduce participants to the concepts of responsible assertion and assertion training.

What is Assertion Training?

Assertion training is a semi-structured training approach which is characterized by its emphasis on acquiring assertive skills through practice. It is a way to manage social conflict which subsequently increases self-esteem. It is basically derived from the school of psychotherapy called Behavioral Therapy. To put it very simply, inadequate behavior leads to negative feelings about oneself which in turn lead to low self-esteem. This creates a cycle in which low self-esteem most likely will lead to inadequate behavior and negative feelings. (Drawing the illustration below on newsprint and then changing "inadequate" to "adequate," "negative" to "positive," and "lower" to "higher" self-esteem, will graphically illustrate the impact of changing behavior.)

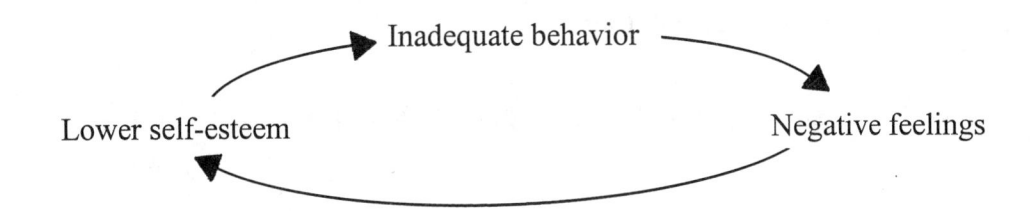

```
         →  Inadequate behavior  ↘
Lower self-esteem                  Negative feelings
         ↖                        ↙
```

Assertion training strives to break the cycle by teaching people adequate behavior which leads to positive feelings and higher self-esteem.

Responsible assertion, as used in this workshop, means that we wish our rights to be respected in making our assertions, we also respect the rights of others. To this end, the teachings, exercises, and role plays stress resolution of interpersonal conflicts rather than winning or getting our way when there is disagreement.

Defined more specifically, **responsible assertion means being able to express your feelings, make free choices, and meet more of your personal needs without experiencing undue guilt or anxiety and without violating the rights and dignity of others.**

How can you tell if you have been assertive? If you have doubts, ask yourself whether a specific behavior increased your self-esteem even slightly. If it did, it was assertive.

Do not forget that being assertive does not necessarily mean getting your way. For example, one person who completed the assertion training workshop reported that she had been playing tennis with a partner who reached over the net to her side in order to return the ball. Finally she spoke up and said, "I believe it's against the rules to return the ball before it crosses the net." I asked her, "Did he stop?" "Oh, no," she replied,

Session 1

"he kept on hitting the ball the same way. But I felt so good at being able to say he was wrong. I never could have said it before!"

Becoming assertive is a goal for which to strive. Just as there are few completely self-actualized persons, there are few completely assertive persons. There may be persons with whom we have difficulty being assertive or situations which need continuing effort. However, as long as we proceed in small steps and feel ourselves increasing in self-esteem, we will feel better about ourselves and have greater control of our lives.

A word of warning: assertion training is not a cure-all. It will not solve all your problems. Because assertion training uses educational techniques, it is not therapy, although there are therapeutic benefits to becoming assertive. Assertion training alone is not likely to help people who are experiencing the loss of a job, or the effects of a divorce or death. Assertion training will not help you learn to make decisions or overcome phobias from the past. There is no time during the session to go in-depth with one person's problems. These crises are best resolved in one-to-one personal counseling prior to entering an assertion training workshop.

This workshop will include four training steps:

❋❋❋❋❋❋❋❋❋❋❋❋❋❋❋❋❋❋❋❋❋❋❋❋❋❋❋❋❋❋❋❋❋

(Workbook p. 5)

Training Steps

- Learning to distinguish assertive from aggressive, nonassertive, and nonassertive-aggressive behaviors.
- Identifying personal rights and accepting them as well as respecting the rights of others.
- Reducing blocks to acting assertively.
- Developing skills through role playing and practice.

❋❋❋❋❋❋❋❋❋❋❋❋❋❋❋❋❋❋❋❋❋❋❋❋❋❋❋❋❋❋❋❋

The first few sessions will include practice using situations that I will specify. During the last few sessions, we will practice situations with which you have difficulty.

In addition, you will be asked to practice certain situations outside the workshop, but only after we have tried them here. I'd like you to record the effects of your practice briefly in the Daily Log included in the workbook. If there are any other incidents which occur in which you acted assertively, aggressively, nonassertively, or nonassertive-aggressively, record them also. I would like you to identify patterns of behavior and also to keep a record of whatever progress you make.

Finally, if you have allowed others to make decisions for you or if you have been willing to do almost anything that a spouse or friend demanded, you may find that they may be shocked and displeased by your new behavior, at least initially. Therefore, it is recommended that you inform your friends and family that you are learning to behave more assertively. The reading, "Dealing with Disapproval" (Workbook, p. 32), should be very helpful. In addition, you might invite your friends and family to examine some of your materials and to help you with constructive feedback when you practice your new behaviors.

Session 1

Exercise: Introductions
(20 minutes)

Purpose: To introduce participants to each other; to provide practice in being assertive.

Introduction: Discuss the exercise as follows:

> *In most groups when people first get together, there is a time when each person, in turn, tells who they are and a few things about themselves. We will do that also. This is a good way to begin to practice being assertive.*
>
> *When it is your turn, say your name. Say it so everyone hears you. Then say some things that will help tell who you are. Because we are still pretty much strangers, you shouldn't expect to tell very personal things about yourself or your innermost secrets; that wouldn't be appropriate. However, it is appropriate to tell where you are from, what you are doing now, why you are in the group, and what interests you.*
>
> *It is assertive to look at people when you talk, not at the floor, or the ceiling, or out the window. Let your gaze fall on different people as you introduce yourself.*
>
> *Before you speak, take a few minutes to think of what to say and then visualize yourself saying it assertively to the group (covert rehearsal).*

Procedure: Start the exercise by introducing yourself, then have each participant do the same.

After each person speaks, give positive feedback on at least one assertive component in that person's delivery (e.g., eye contact, body language, voice control, pitch, conciseness). Invite the other participants to give positive comments also.

Notes:

Discussion: Workshop Expectations and Procedures

The following outline provides an introduction to the assertion training workshop for participants. Listed below are goals, objectives, training methods, and techniques and expectations for both leaders and participants. Review these with the participants and answer any questions they may have. This material is provided in the participant workbook and is assigned reading for this session's homework.

✻✻✻✻✻✻✻✻✻✻✻✻✻✻✻✻✻✻✻✻✻✻✻✻✻✻✻✻

(📄 Workbook p. 6)

Workshop Expectations and Procedures

General Goal: This introductory level workshop will help participants explore the concept of assertive behavior and will include methods and opportunities to practice assertive behaviors.

Objectives: Based on attendance and participation in all six sessions of the workshop, it is expected you will:

- make a self-assessment of the interpersonal situations in which you would like to be more assertive (📄 Workbook p. 4);
- be able to verbally distinguish among assertive, aggressive, nonassertive, and nonassertive-aggressive (NAG) behaviors;
- examine and clarify your beliefs about interpersonal rights related to assertive behavior;
- be able to describe how certain emotions are created which make it difficult to be assertive but easy to be aggressive or non-assertive;
- have several opportunities to practice standing up for your opinions and needs without violating the rights of others.

Methods and Techniques: The primary methods used to present the material include: mini-lectures, discussions, demonstrations of concepts, questionnaires, homework assignments, and behavioral rehearsals. Sessions will focus on behaviors such as dealing with criticism and "put-downs," persistence, asking for favors, refusing requests, and expressing opinions. Specific techniques to be discussed and practiced include: fogging (desensitization), the broken record technique (persistence), workable compromise, negative assertion, negative inquiry, and self-disclosure ("I" language).

Workshop Format: This is a workshop with an educational format. This is not group psychotherapy. If you are currently experiencing intense personal anguish or frustration or if you find it difficult to hold your life together, then this group is not the place to begin. The workshop is brief and does not permit in-depth work with any given individual. As a result, your frustration and pain, in all likelihood, would be

Session 1

heightened — leading to less effective interpersonal behavior. It is recommended that you start with one-to-one counseling, and if you desire, later enroll in an assertiveness workshop.

Participation: You are free to refuse to participate in any activity you choose. No reasons need to be provided for declining to be involved in any activity, suggestions, or exercises. If you choose not to follow the group leader's suggestions, you are expected to do so in a manner that does not interfere with the choices and participation of other members.

Expectations for Participants:

- All participants are asked to keep a daily log of situations in which they used assertive, non-assertive, and aggressive behavior.
- A homework assignment will be given each session.
- Participation in each group will include doing role plays and exercises, some of which require paper and pencil.
- The participants are expected to attend each session.
- Any information shared during the discussions of the group will be kept confidential by participants.

Expectations for Workshop Leader(s):

- The leader(s) will use educational and training skills to teach assertive behavior. This is not group therapy.
- The leader(s) will provide within the session for the practice of assertive skills.
- The leader(s) will teach skills to reduce blocks to assertive behavior.
- The leader(s) will be prepared, will model assertive behavior, and will be present every week.
- The leader(s) will keep confidential all information shared during group discussions.

✳✳✳✳✳✳✳✳✳✳✳✳✳✳✳✳✳✳✳✳✳✳✳✳✳✳✳✳✳✳✳

Session 1

Exercise: Ice-Breaker — Do You Like Artichokes?
(5 minutes)

Purpose: To help participants relax by doing a non-threatening exercise; to make it easier for participants to respond to each other and the leaders.

Procedure: Ask the participants to imagine a line representing a continuum of one to 10. Mark two locations in the room.

State that one point represents 1 (meaning "not at all"), while the other point represents 10 (meaning "a great deal").

Ask the participants to place themselves on the line according to how well they like the following items. Ask each of the questions below:

- (?) "How well do you like artichokes?"
- (?) "How well do you like asparagus?"
- (?) "How well do you like the color purple?"
- (?) "How well do you like the color yellow?"
- (?) "How well do you like Chinese food?"
- (?) "How well do you like Italian food?"
- (?) "How well do you like big cities?"
- (?) "How well do you like small towns?"
- (?) "How well do you like _____?" (Leader may fill in the blank.)
- (?) "How assertive do you rate yourself?"

Notes:

Session 1

Exercise: I Need to Think About That...
(15 minutes)

Purpose: To help participants act assertively in situations where they are unsure of what they think or what they want to do.

Introduction: Discuss the exercise as follows:

Being able to choose the time, place, and person for an assertive action is half the battle. However, more often persons make requests or ask opinions for which we are not prepared. For some reason, we tend to feel that we must make an instant decision or an immediate reply, even though we are confused, uncertain, or just plain ignorant as to what our response should be. Usually, we respond in one of two ways: with a hasty decision or opinion we regret immediately afterward; or with an awkward period of hemming and hawing. In either case we feel we should have responded better.

If you do not know what you think or want to do, the assertive way to handle this situation is to express your uncertainty and ask for more time or take more time to consider the request or question.

Procedure: Divide the group into pairs.

Ask one person in each pair to make five to 10 requests or ask questions requiring a response (not "How are you?"). Some examples are:

- ⁇ "Would you lend me your car?"
- ⁇ "How about dinner tonight?"
- ⁇ "What do you think about the economic situation?"
- ⁇ "What are you going to do about fixing the refrigerator?"
- ⁇ "What do you think about Mary's proposal?"
- ⁇ "How would you tell an employee he or she is not performing adequately?"

Ask the second person to imagine himself or herself responding assertively with "I'm not sure, I need a few minutes to think about it." Then have him or her say that and only that to every single question.

Have the participants reverse roles and repeat the steps described above.

Notes:

Session 1

Discussion: Behaviors Defined and Explored

Learning to distinguish among different kinds of behavior is important. Discuss the following definitions and examples of each behavior with the participants so that they can begin to learn the differences. Discuss the questions and answers provided and ask for further questions from participants.

✳✳✳✳✳✳✳✳✳✳✳✳✳✳✳✳✳✳✳✳✳✳✳✳✳✳✳✳✳✳

(📄 Workbook p. 8)

Behaviors Defined and Explored*

Nonassertive Behavior**

Definition: Nonassertive behavior means failing to express honest feelings, thoughts, or beliefs and consequently permitting others to take advantage of you, or expressing your thoughts and feelings in an apologetic, cautious, or unconfident manner so that other people disregard them.

Examples: When you let someone talk you into something you do not want to do, such as going to a movie you do not want to see, even though you have already mentioned your dislike of it ("I don't like violent movies, but OK.").

When you are criticized for your work but you never give your side.

When your husband brings home unexpected guests for dinner continually and you never say anything.

Message: "I don't count. You can take advantage of me. My feelings do not matter — only yours do. My thoughts are not worth listening to, only yours are important. I'm nothing. You are superior."

Respect: You show respect only for the other person's needs and rights. You have no respect for your own rights.

Some Reasons You May Behave in a Nonassertive Way:

- You mistake assertion for aggression. You think that being assertive is being aggressive or hostile.

- You mistake nonassertion for politeness. You think that to be tactful and polite you have to be nonassertive.

- You do not believe in your rights.

---
*This material is also assigned reading for this session's homework.
**Adapted with permission from E.P. Kirchner and R.E. Kennedy, *Leaders Manual for an Assertive Skills Course in Correctional Settings*, (Institute for Research on Human Resources: University Park, PA: Pennsylvania State University, 1978).

Session 1

- You are afraid of what will happen if you are assertive.
- You may lack skills. You do not know how to be assertive.
- You hope to gain a certain type of response from another person (Unspoken Bargain).

Nonassertive Behavior (The Unspoken Bargain)*

I won't assert myself when you:	**In exchange for your:**
(Boyfriend) . . . constantly talk about your past girlfriends, only socialize with your friends, ridicule my opinions.	(Boyfriend) . . . dating only me, changing these objectionable behaviors without my having to ask you to.
(Husband) . . . make me the scapegoat for your business frustrations, give me the "silent" treatment, are abrupt in sex.	(Husband) . . . staying married to me and maintaining our home.
(Employer) . . . constantly ask me to work on my lunch hour for no extra pay, unfairly criticize me.	(Employer) . . . giving me a raise without my having to ask for it, never firing me.

Consequences of Nonassertive Behavior — your fear of what would happen if you are assertive may be reduced or avoided, but. . .

- You may lose respect and self-respect, and feel hurt and anxious.
- You may become angry at yourself and at other persons, but keep this anger "inside" (sometimes causing "explosions" later).
- Others may take advantage of you.
- You may not receive what is rightfully yours or receive it in a devious or immature way.
- The other person may feel irritation or pity toward you and may feel guilty.

Aggressive Behavior**

Definition: Aggressive behavior means standing up for your rights and expressing your thoughts, feelings, and beliefs in ways that are dishonest, usually inappropriate, and violate the rights of the other person. The goal is domination and winning — forcing the other person to lose by humiliating, degrading, belittling, insulting, or overpowering him or her so that the person becomes weaker and

---

*With permission from P. Jakubowski, "Facilitating the Growth of Women Through Assertive Training," *Counseling Psychologist* 4, no. 1, 1973.

** Adapted with permission from E.P. Kirchner and R.E. Kennedy, *Leaders Manual for an Assertive Skills Course in Correctional Settings,* (Institute for Research on Human Resources: University Park, Penn.: Pennsylvania State University, 1978).

becomes less able to express and defend his or her rights and needs.

Example: Statements such as: "You just thrive on violence, don't you! Well I'm not like that. I can't stand those movies, there must be something wrong with people who like movies like that!"

"You don't know what you're talking about. I know this project better than you."

Being short and glum through the meal and after the guests are gone, saying, "You are the most inconsiderate, thoughtless person I've ever seen! You never think of me, just selfish, selfish all the time."

Message: "This is what I think; you're stupid for believing differently."

Respect: You show no respect at all for the other person's needs, opinions, or rights. "This is what I want. What you want doesn't count. This is what I feel. What you feel isn't important."

Reasons You May Behave in an Aggressive Way:
- You fear you will not have control over other people unless you act aggressively.
- You feel you will be open to attack if you do not bully the other person.
- You are not assertive enough early in a situation.
- You think that aggression is the only way to get through to other people; the only way to maintain your rights.
- You may be afraid that you look nonassertive or weak.
- You may not know how to be assertive.

Consequences of Aggressive Behavior — you may have success in the short run, but . . .
- You may face retaliation by the other person.
- You may have poor relationships with other people — aggressive people usually help create aggressiveness with other people.
- You may face failures such as the loss of a marriage, loss of a friend, loss of a job, etc.
- You may lose respect from others, who are hurt, embarrassed, angry, or resentful.
- You may feel guilty.

Session 1

Nonassertive-Aggressive (NAG Behavior)

Definition: Nonassertive-Aggressive (NAG) behavior means failing to stand up for yourself initially, then sabotaging the situation later so that the other person feels humiliated, guilty, punished, or angry.

Example: Accepting an invitation but leaving early because of a headache.
Taking longer and doing a sloppy job on work assignments.
Submitting but not responding in sexual intercourse.

Message: "I did what you asked, didn't I? So I can't be punished if it didn't work out."

Respect: You show respect for neither the other person's needs and rights nor your own.

Reasons You May Behave in a NAG Way:
- You believe you have no power and so resort to indirect ways to get what you want.
- You believe there is less risk of reprisal if you are underhanded.
- You do not believe in the other person's rights.
- You lack assertive skills.
- You believe NAG behavior is more polite or feminine.

Consequences of Nonassertive-Aggressive Behavior — your fear about what would happen if you are assertive may be reduced or avoided, but . . .
- You may lose self-respect because you get your way by being underhanded.
- You may waste time and energy by being devious.
- Your relationships may be damaged.

Assertive Behavior*

Definition: Assertive behavior means standing up for personal rights and expressing thoughts, feelings, and beliefs in direct, honest, and appropriate ways that do not violate another's rights.

Examples: "I've decided not to see violent movies any more. Let's find another we can both enjoy or do something else tonight."

"I've spent a lot of time researching this project. Can you tell me which parts you don't like and we'll go over it together."

---
*Adapted with permission from E.P. Kitchner and R.E. Kennedy, *Leader's Manual for an Assertive Skills Course in Correctional Settings,* (University Park, Penn.: Pennsylvania State University, 1978).

"When you bring home guests unexpectedly and I have to improvise or skimp with servings, I get very upset and frustrated. Next time you do, please call me at least an hour ahead of time."

Message: "This is what I think. This is what I feel. This is how I see the situation." The message expresses "who you are" and is said without dominating, humiliating, or offending the other person.

Respect: Assertion involves respect, not deference. Deference is acting in a subservient, undignified manner as though the other person is right or better just because he or she is older, more powerful, more experienced, or of a different class, race, or sex. Deference means expressing yourself in ways that are apologetic, appeasing, or that do not show respect for your worth. Assertion involves respect for expressing your needs and your rights.

Some Reasons You May Behave in an Assertive Way:
- You know how to be assertive; one way or another you have picked up assertive techniques.
- You have control over yourself.
- You are confident about yourself.
- You have self-respect.
- You respect your rights.
- You respect the rights of others.

Consequences of Assertive Behavior
- You can maintain mature relationships with other people.
- You can increase your percentage of success.
- Needless fear, anger, and guilt can be prevented.
- You can gain respect from others.
- You can feel in control, confident, and self-respecting.
- Other people feel valued and respected.

How Can you Tell When You are Nonassertive or Aggressive?

You are nonassertive when you. . . .
- Do not stand up for your rights.
- Let other people take unfair advantage of you.
- Do not express your views and feelings.
- Feel guilty when you do stand up for your rights or express your feelings.
- Are unable to make reasonable requests of other people.

Session 1

- Are unable to start or carry on conversations comfortably.
- Are unable to recognize and express your good points.
- Feel badly about yourself after experiencing any of the above.

You are aggressive when you . . .
- Ignore another person's rights.
- Take unfair advantage of other people.
- Make other people look or feel stupid, small, or afraid.
- Become abusive when you are angry with someone or when you are criticizing someone.
- Make unreasonable demands or other people.
- Monopolize conversations.
- Brag obnoxiously and make unrealistic claims about your good points.
- Feel good at first but guilty later as a result of any of the above behaviors.

You are appropriately assertive when you . . .
- Stand up for your own rights and let other people do the same.
- Can say "no" when you do not want to say "yes" to someone's request.
- Can express your positive feelings about other people and what they do.
- Can express negative feelings about other people and what they do without being abusive or cruel.
- Can receive compliments without denying them.
- Can take criticism without becoming defensive.
- Can start and carry on conversations.
- Can recognize and express your good points.
- Can ask for what is rightfully yours.
- Feel good about yourself and in control of yourself after experiencing any of the above.

Does being appropriately assertive mean you "win" or get your way all the time?

No. Often it means you compromise, but do not feel you have "lost." Often it means you increase your chances to work things out to your satisfaction at a later time even if you are not satisfied completely now.

Does "expressing your views and feelings" mean you say whatever is on your mind? Do you just let your emotions go all the time, with everyone?

No. For example, you may get temporary satisfaction if you tell the boss to "go to hell," but the long-range effect could be losing your job.

Should I always be assertive?

This is up to you. You are free to choose not to assert yourself.

How do I decide when to be assertive?

When trying to decide whether or not to be assertive, ask yourself three questions:

- How important is this to me?
- How will I feel afterward?
- How much will it cost me? (Do not scare yourself with irrational assumptions or unlikely probabilities. Be realistic.)

Other definitions of appropriately assertive behavior...

Assertive behavior involves the honest and straightforward expression of feelings, done in a socially acceptable manner. It satisfies you and at the same time is effective socially.

When you are appropriately assertive, you assert your identity. You express by your words and actions — this is what I think, this is what I feel, this is what I am.

✻✻✻✻✻✻✻✻✻✻✻✻✻✻✻✻✻✻✻✻✻✻✻✻✻✻✻✻✻✻

Exercise: Discrimination
(20 minutes)

Purpose: To identify the participants' misunderstandings about assertive, aggressive and nonassertive behavior; to help them correct their misunderstandings.

Introduction: Review the definitions of behavior with the group using several examples. Discuss the exercise with the participants as follows:

> *Now we are going to listen to a series of statements revolving around a situation. The statement may be aggressive, assertive, NAG, or nonassertive. I will ask each of you, in turn, to share your private decision. Don't go by majority rule in making up your mind. I'm particularly interested in those who see the statement differently from the rest of the group because this will give me a chance to clear up whatever confusion may exist about these different behaviors.*

Procedure: Read aloud the following situation:

Situation 1: Aunt Margaret, with whom you prefer not to spend time, is on the telephone. She has just told you of her plans to spend three weeks visiting you, beginning next week. Your response is:

Session 1

A. You think, "Oh, no!" but say, "We'd love to have you come and stay as long as you like." However, during her visit you are cross and complain constantly. (nonassertive-aggressive)

B. You tell her the children have just come down with bad colds, and the spare bed has a broken bedspring and you'll be going to Cousin Bill's the weekend after next, none of which is true. (nonassertive)

C. You say, "We'll be glad to have you come for the weekend, but we simply cannot invite you for longer. A short visit is happier for everyone, and we'll want to see each other again sooner if we keep it brief." (assertive)

Ask the participants to identify the situation as aggressive, assertive, NAG, or nonassertive. If a participant misidentifies a situation, start the discussion by saying "What was it about the response that caused you to see it as . . . ?" Other questions to ask are:

(?) "How do others see it?"

(?) "Are you saying to yourself that someone wouldn't like you?"

(?) "Aren't you assuming that everybody reacts like you do?"

Repeat the above steps for each of the following situations.

Situation 2: At the barbershop, the stylist has just finished cutting your hair and turns the chair toward the mirror so that you can inspect his or her work. You feel that you would like the sides trimmed more. Your response is:

A. Sarcastically you say, "You sure didn't take much off the sides, did you?" (aggressive)

B. You say, "I'd like to have the sides trimmed more." (assertive)

C. You either nod your head in assent, or say "That's OK," or say nothing. (nonassertive)

Situation 3: You have made a mistake on some aspect of your job. Your supervisor discovers it and is letting you know rather harshly that you should not have been so careless. Your response is:

A. You over-apologize, saying "I'm really sorry. I'm so stupid, it was really silly of me. I'll never let it happen again. I am really dumb." (nonassertive)

B. You bristle and say, "You have no right to criticize my work whatsoever, especially after all the mistakes he makes that you correct for him. How about everybody else's mistakes. You never criticize them like this." (aggressive)

C. You say, "Yes, that was a mistake. I'm sorry about it and will be more careful next time, although I feel you are somewhat harsh." (assertive)

Situation 4: You are in a lecture with 300 other students. The professor speaks softly and you know that many others are having the same trouble hearing him. Your response is:

A. You raise your hand, get the professor's attention and ask, "Would you mind speaking louder?" (assertive)

B. You yell out, "Speak up! Can't hear you!" (aggressive)

C. You continue to strain to hear and eventually move close to the front of the room, but say nothing about the too-soft voice. (nonassertive)

Situation 5: At a party where you don't know anyone except the host, you want to circulate and get to know others. You walk up to three people who are talking. Your response is:

A. You stand close to them and smile but say nothing, waiting for them to notice you. (nonassertive)

B. You wait for a pause in the conversation, introduce yourself and comment on the subject. (assertive)

C. You listen to the subject they are talking about, then break in and state, "I disagree with your point of view." (aggressive)

Notes:

Session 1

Exercise: Subjective Unit of Disturbance Scale*
(SUDS Score)
(10 minutes)

Purpose: To help participants become aware of and be able to communicate their subjectively-experienced levels of anxiety.

Procedure: Read the following to the participants:

> *Imagine a scene where you are completely relaxed and calm. For some people this may be while lying on a sunny beach or beside a pool. For others, this occurs while reading a good book or fishing.*
>
> *Give your feelings in the most relaxed situation a score of "0."*
>
> *Next, imagine a situation where you are completely panic stricken. It may be in speaking before a large group or taking an exam. Your hands may be clammy, you feel shaky, and you feel anxious and constricted.*
>
> *Give the feeling you experience in this situation a rating of "100."*
>
> *You have now identified the two-end points of the Subjective Unit of Disturbance Scale (SUDS): 0 and 100. Imagine the entire scale (like a ruler) going from 0 SUDS (completely relaxed), to 100 SUDS (extremely anxious).*

❋❋❋❋❋❋❋❋❋❋❋❋❋❋❋❋❋❋❋❋❋❋❋❋❋❋❋❋❋❋❋❋

(Workbook p. 5)

Subjective Units of Disturbance Scale

0	10	20	30	40	50	60	70	80	90	100
completely relaxed										**extremely anxious**

❋❋❋❋❋❋❋❋❋❋❋❋❋❋❋❋❋❋❋❋❋❋❋❋❋❋❋❋❋❋❋❋

What is your present SUDS level?

After the participants have indicated their SUDS level, yell loudly and directly at a participant: "What is it now! This very minute!" (The participant usually responds

---
*With permission from Wolpe, J., *The Practice of Behavior Therapy*, (New York: Pergamon Press, 1982).

Session 1

with a much higher SUDS level, demonstrating that people can easily discriminate between high and low SUDS levels.)

Discussion: Discuss the SUDS scale with the participants as follows:

The SUDS scale will be used throughout the assertion-training program. After responding to each situation in which you have practiced assertive behavior, note your SUDS score in your log. A goal of repeated assertive practice is to lower your anxiety as much as possible. However, there are certain situations or certain people who will always create some anxiety. For example, expressing justified annoyance to your boss is usually an anxiety-producing experience. Therefore, your goal is not to reduce your SUDS level to zero or 10 in all situations, but to reduce your SUDS level to where you feel comfortable enough to express yourself. High levels of anxiety are unpleasant for most people. Moreover, the anxiety can inhibit you from saying what you want and can interfere with the way you deliver your message.

Notes:

Session 1

Exercise: Body Language
(20 minutes)

Purpose: To stimulate the participants' awareness of those nonverbal behaviors which influence their first impressions; to stimulate consideration of nonverbal behaviors which participants might choose to change during the group sessions; to teach participants to give specific behavioral feedback; to stimulate awareness of participants' ability to talk about "nothing."

Materials: Newsprint, marking pens, slips of paper with topics listed (enough for each participant.)

Procedure: Say to the participants:

There are many ways that people can communicate nonassertively, even though the verbal message may be assertive. I can say the same words, "It's your turn to do the dishes," and you may receive three different messages.

List them on the newsprint.

Suggestions: When demonstrating:

aggressive behavior — stand closer, stare at the other person, speak louder, clench fists, or shake finger;

nonassertive behavior — stand further apart, body turned away slightly, soft voice, hesitant speech, wring hands, look down, mumble;

assertive — stand at comfortable distance, about three feet, look directly at person, hands relaxed, body relaxed, speak clearly and firmly.

Notes:

Session 1

Exercise: Absurd Topics
(20 minutes)

Purpose: To sharpen participants' perceptions of nonverbal behavior.

Procedure: Write topics on slips of paper (such as lint, pins, watches, eyebrows, Kleenex, etc.)

Ask the participants to form groups of three and randomly select an absurd topic. Have one person in the group act as timekeeper; the second as listener to the monologue, and the third as speaker. Have each participant talk for 60 seconds about his or her topic.

Ask the listeners to identify the nonverbal behaviors that are effectively holding their attention. Use the newsprint list as a check.

After all three persons have spoken, make sure that each receives positive feedback on what the others liked about the speaker's nonverbal behaviors.

Ask the participants to think about their behavior. Ask if there is any behavior they would like to change.

Suggestions: Make sure the feedback focuses on how the participant behaved (nonverbal behavior) rather than on what the participant said.

When feedback is given after each participant talks, the speakers are likely to imitate the previous speaker and feel anxious about doing as well or better. By waiting until all three have spoken, they realize the positive feedback is for natural behavior.

If participants report feeling silly doing this exercise, tell them to give themselves permission to do something silly or to be imperfect.

Notes:

Session 1

Exercise: Desensitization to Eye Contact
(5 minutes)

Purpose: To help participants learn how to maintain eye contact in social situations.

Introduction: Discuss eye contact as follows:

Let's do a short exercise on eye contact since so many nonassertive people have trouble with that. If you have this problem, it probably started when you were two and could not understand language. At that age, it must have seemed like a huge person in a loud voice pointed two large light beams that saw way down to your soul and boomed, "Who did that?" You looked away and hoped you were invisible. This exercise helps to desensitize you to that early fear.

Procedure: Have the participants pick a partner and face him or her in a position four feet apart. Most social exchanges take place at that distance.

Tell the participants to look at their partner's right ankle, left knee, right hip, breast bone, left shoulder, right shoulder, chin, left ear, right ear, forehead, right temple, and finally, into his or her eyes.

Next, have the participants look into their partner's eyes, and very slowly start looking away. Ask the partner to sit with his or her hand at shoulder level and raise a finger as soon as she or he can tell when their eyes are out of contact.

Discussion: Say to the participants:

For those of you who have a difficult time initiating and maintaining eye contact, you will notice that at a distance of four feet, a person cannot tell whether you are looking him or her in the eye or in the ear. Talk to their ears or forehead if it helps you to feel more comfortable.

Notes:

Session 1

Beginning and Ending the Session

After the first introductory session, succeeding sessions might start with discussion of the homework assignment or behavior that participants chose to practice between sessions. Success should be genuinely rewarded. Focus on the participants' ability to evaluate their assertiveness as opposed to judging their behavior. When participants cite situations they feel were not handled well, focus discussion on clarifying their personal rights, what kept them from being assertive, and what they would like to do.

After making homework assignments, you may close the session by doing "The Link" exercise. The Link provides closure to the session, helps integrate the exercises and cognitive material, and is useful for purposes of evaluation. It takes about 5 minutes.

Exercise: The Link
(5 minutes)

Purpose: To help participants integrate the exercises and cognitive material; to allow evaluation by the leader.

Introduction: Discuss the exercise as follows:

Take a few minutes to think about today's session and complete the phrase which best summarizes your feelings. We will go around the group so that each person has a turn.

Procedure: Ask the participants to turn to the chart in their workbooks.

✱✱✱✱✱✱✱✱✱✱✱✱✱✱✱✱✱✱✱✱✱✱✱✱✱✱✱✱✱✱✱✱

(Workbook p. 5)

The Link

Today I learned that . . .	I wish that . . .
Right now I feel . . .	I was pleased . . .
This session helped me to . . .	I will think more about . . .
What I like about myself is . . .	Next time I'd like to . . .

✱✱✱✱✱✱✱✱✱✱✱✱✱✱✱✱✱✱✱✱✱✱✱✱✱✱✱✱✱✱✱✱

Have each participant complete a phrase.

Session 1

Suggestions: The phrases included in the workbook are all assertive and can also be used in classroom and other interpersonal situations to express opinions and needs.

Notes:

Homework

Readings:
- 📖 Workshop Expectations and Procedures (📄 Workbook p. 6)
- 📖 Behaviors Defined and Explored (📄 Workbook p. 8)
- 📖 Is Being Assertive Being Selfish (📄 Workbook p. 15)

Activities:
- ☑ Keep a daily log. Record how you or others behave following the sample entry provided. Log sheets are found at the end of the workbook. At this point, you are learning to identify the different kinds of behaviors — not to practice them. Observe three situations.
- ☑ Do the Discrimination Test (📄 Workbook p. 16)
- ☑ Introduce yourself to three strangers. Record your behavior in your Daily Log.
- ☑ Respond to requests with "I need to think about that." Record the results in your Daily Log.

(Workbook p. 15)

Homework Reading: Is Being Assertive Being Selfish?

If you do not think you are worth loving why should anyone else think so? People who love themselves and know they deserve the good things in life (and strive for them) are usually able to be most generous and giving to others. If you really believe in your own self-worth, you are free to serve others without expecting anything in return. Such "selfish" people do not complain if they are not appreciated. Because they appreciate themselves, they are not self-centered, and can devote large chunks of their lives to others.

People respect strength, not weakness. In fact, you will find that others would much rather be around you if you like yourself because you do not make them responsible for your happiness. In addition, you can teach others to take responsibility for their lives by setting a good example.

If you do not love yourself very much, it is almost impossible to be nice to others. You become a complaining, tiresome person, begging for recognition from those you have elevated above yourself.

Homework Activity: Discrimination Test*

(Workbook p. 16)

N – Nonassertive
A – Assertive
AG – Aggressive
NAG – Nonassertive/Aggressive

Situation:

1. A good friend calls and tells you she desperately needs you to canvass the street for a charity.

2. You are at a meeting of seven men and one woman. At the beginning of the meeting the chairman asks you to be the secretary. You respond,

3. You are team teaching, but you are doing all the planning, teaching, interacting, and evaluating students. You say,

4. The bus is crowded with high school students who are talking to their friends. You want to get off but no one pays attention when you say "Out please." Finally you say,

5. A student comes late to class for the third time. The teacher responds,

6. A man asks you for a date. You have dated him once before and you are not interested in dating him again.

7. The local library calls and asks you to return a book which you never checked out. You respond,

8. You are in a line at the store. Someone behind you has one item, and asks to get in front of you. You respond.

Response

You do not want to do it and say, "Oh gee, Fran, I just know that Jerry will be mad at me if I say "Yes." He says I'm always getting involved in too many things. You know how Jerry is about things like this."

"No, I'm sick and tired of being the secretary just because I'm the only woman in the group."

"On paper we are team teaching and yet I see that I am doing all the work. I'd like to talk about changing this."

"What is the matter with you kids? I'm supposed to get off at the next corner."

"I'm really bothered when you're not here at the beginning of my lecture. It is difficult for me to make the lecture understandable if you are not here from the beginning."

You say, "Are you sure you want to go out with me? I'm not sure about my schedule."

"What are you talking about? You people better get your records straight — I never had that book and don't you try to make me pay for it."

"I realize that you don't want to wait in line, but I was here first and I really would like to get out of here."

---

*Reprinted and adapted with permission from A. Lange and P. Jakubowski, *Responsible Assertive Behavior: Cognitive-Behavioral Procedures for Trainees*, (Champaign, Ill.: Research Press, 1976).

N – Nonassertive
A – Asserttive
AG – Aggressive
NAG – Nonassertive/Aggressive

Situation:

9. A parent is talking with a married child on the telephone and would like the child to come for a visit. When the child politely refuses, the parent says,

10. An employer sends a memorandum stating that there should be no more toll business calls made without first getting prior permission. One employee responds,

11. Your husband expects dinner on the table when he arrives home from work and becomes angry when it is not there immediately. You respond,

12. Plans to vacation together are abruptly changed by a friend and reported to you on the phone. You respond,

13. A parent is reprimanding the children when they haven't cleaned up their room and says,

14. Your roommate habitually leaves the room a mess. You say,

15. You husband wants to watch a football game on TV. There is something else that you'd like to watch. You say,

16. A parent is annoyed that the school counselor has not done anything about the son's conflict with a teacher. The parent says,

17. Your supervisor has just berated you for your work. You respond,

18. Your 10-year-old child has interrupted you three times with something that is not urgent. You have assertively asked her not to interrupt you. The child has again interrupted you. You say,

Response

"You're never available when I need you. All you ever think about is yourself."

"You're taking away my professional judgment. I'm insulted."

"I feel awful about dinner. I know you're tired and hungry . . . it's all my fault. I've been so busy today, the kids were rotten . . . ."

"Wow, this has really taken me by surprise. I'd like to call you back after I've had some time to digest what's happened."

"You've got to be the worst kids in the whole city! If I had known parenthood was going to be like this, I would never have had any kids at all!"

"You're a mess and our room is a mess."

"Well, ah, honey, go ahead and watch the game. I guess I could do some ironing." (Then you talk constantly through the whole game.)

"I have asked the school to investigate the situation in my son's classroom and it concerns me that nothing has been done. I must insist that this situation be looked into."

"I think some of your criticisms are true, but I would have liked your being less personal about telling me about my shortcomings."

"I can't listen to you and talk on the phone at the same time. I'll be on the phone a few more minutes and then we'll talk."

✻ ✻

Session 1

Key for Discrimination Test

1. N
2. Ag
3. A
4. Ag
5. A
6. N
7. Ag
8. A
9. Ag
10. Ag
11. N
12. A
13. Ag
14. Ag
15. NAG
16. A
17. A
18. A

(📖 Workbook p. 19)

Homework Activity: Sample Daily Log of Assertive Behavior*

Date	Behavior	Person	Satisfactory Aspects of Performance	Aspects of Performance that Needs Improvement	Overall Evaluation (Excellent/Good/Fair/Poor) SUDS Score	My Behavior Appropriately: Non-aggressive Assertive
Sample Entry 1/04/85	Refused Request	Mary (spouse)	Eye contact	Content, sarcasm	Poor SUDS score #90	Aggressive

*Reproduction master for Daily Log is provided in Appendix B.

31

Session 2
Respecting Rights

Overview

Goal: To help participants learn to value their personal rights and those of others.

Materials: 8-1/2" x 11" paper or cardboard with a personal right written on each, blank 8-1/2" x 11" paper or cardboard, marking pens, tape, packet of securities for each participant

Contents: Homework Review
Exercise: Making Positive Self-Statements
Mini-Lecture: Rights and Responsibilities
Discussion: Personal Rights
Exercise: Others' Rights
Exercise: Rights Auction
Exercise: Rights Role Play
Closing the Session
Homework
    📖 Reading: Irrational Beliefs
    ☑ Activities: Exercises in Concreteness
           Use of Rights Won in Auction
           Three Positive Self-Statements to Others
           Daily Log

Session 2

Homework Review
(15 minutes)

All sessions should start with a homework review. You may wish to use the format suggested below. Since the format is the same for each session, this page will not be repeated.

1. Review homework while the group is gathering during the first 15 minutes of the session.

2. Check the daily logs. Were incidents recorded correctly? If time is short, you may wish to collect the logs to review and to comment upon in writing. Extra copies of the log sheets are provided in the workbook.

3. Ask for the participants' reactions to the homework assignments. Ask questions such as:
   - ⍰ "How did you feel when you introduced yourself to strangers?"
   - ⍰ "How did you feel when you said 'I need to think about that'?"
   - ⍰ "What were other folks' reactions to you?"
   - ⍰ "Did you have any problems recognizing the different kinds of behavior?"

4. Provide the correct answers for the Discrimination Test. Discuss any items which the participants may question.

5. Ask for reports of successful assertion. Remind the participants that at this joint being able to speak up when they want to is the goal and that successful assertion does not necessarily mean that they must have "won" or made things happen their way.

6. If participants are not satisfied with their assertive experiences, review the experiences before the group. Ask questions such as:
   - ⍰ "What were the actual words used?"
   - ⍰ "What would you have liked to say?"
   - ⍰ "Could it have been said better?"
   - ⍰ "What was the nonverbal behavior?"
   - ⍰ "Was the situation too complex?"
   - ⍰ "Did the other person react to past behavior rather than new behavior?"
   - ⍰ "Is the participant feeling guilty needlessly?"
   - ⍰ "Why does he or she think the experience was not assertive?"
   - ⍰ "Did the participant give in at the first sign of resistance?"

7. Remind the participants that even if their attempts at being assertive were not successful, they should be proud of their efforts to speak up making their thoughts and wishes known.

Session 2

Exercise: Making Positive Self-Statements
(5 minutes)

Introduction: Discuss making self-statements as follows:

Think of at least two or three things about yourself in which you take pride. They should be things for which you would be willing to receive compliments. They should be things that you feel are good about yourself.

For example, think about your appearance, your personality, your abilities, your accomplishments, whatever. Here is a chance to get some practice in asserting positive things about yourself. Honestly compliment yourself. Take a minute to think about your positive self-statements and then imagine yourself saying them assertively to the group.

Procedure: State: "I'll lead off. It's easier for me because I've had some time to think about it and many opportunities to practice this skill."

Start the activity by making two positive self-statements about yourself. Then have the participants do the same.

Discussion: Discuss the following questions with the participants after all have spoken:

- (?) "Why is it so hard to say anything nice about ourselves?"
- (?) "How did we learn this?"
- (?) "Why is it necessary to sometimes be able to make positive self-statements (job interviews, volunteering, social relationships)."
- (?) "Why should anyone like you or believe in you if you do not even like or believe in yourself?"

Notes:

Session 2

Mini-Lecture: Rights and Responsibilities

The purpose of the following lecture is to introduce participants to the concepts of rights and responsibilities.

Rights

Philosophy of Assertive Behavior

Often people are not sure about how they would like to behave in a particular situation because they are unclear about what rights they have and what rights belong to others. Rights are the affirmation of an individual's values. They are the beliefs that allow us to lead our lives the way we want. They are something we must claim; they are not given to us by someone else.

Often we believe that others have rights, but we do not accept them for ourselves. For example, we may think others have the right to refuse a request, but do not think that we have the same right. I would like to emphasize the fact that no one has a right to take advantage of another human being under any circumstances. For instance, an employer has no right to take advantage of an employee's natural rights to courtesy and respect as a human being; doctors should not feel that they can "talk down" to factory workers. Each person has a right to speak his or her piece, even though he or she may have a limited amount of formal education, or be "from the wrong side of the tracks." All persons are created equal on a human-to-human plane and all deserve the fundamental right to express their opinions, needs, and feelings.

Using Rights

Sometimes other people "put us down" or discount our opinions, needs, or feelings, tempting us to respond nonassertively so that we allow our rights to be violated. Conversely, many people do not believe they have personal rights and so do not act on them. Identifying and accepting these rights help lead to assertive behavior. Assertion, rather than manipulation, submission, or hostility, enriches life and ultimately leads to more satisfying personal relationships with people. Since many (maybe all) actions imply certain personal rights, it is important that we recognize what those personal rights are in order to act on them.

Responsibilities

Having rights does not mean having license to do whatever you want. You must always remember that the other person also has the right to express opinions, make mistakes, etc. Moreover there are responsibilities attached to each right. For example, the responsibilities which accompany the right to make a mistake include acknowledging the fact that a mistake was made, not making the same mistake again and again, and accepting other people's rights to make mistakes. When individuals accept the right to feel and express angry feelings, the attendant responsibilities are (1) to resist being abusive, and (2) to assess whether their anger stems from their own imposed judgmental "shoulds and oughts," or whether another person's behavior has concrete and specific effects which result in more legitimate irritation.

Finally, responsible assertion means not deliberately using personal power to manipulatively intimidate less powerful people in situations where there is conflict.

Conflict of Rights

Quite often, a situation involving two persons will involve a conflict between each person's rights. In instances of this sort, it is important to take a flexible rather than a rigid stance. Can some compromise be equitably worked out or is it a situation which involves personal integrity and is not appropriate for compromise?

Finally, while we can expect to be treated with respect, and we usually are, there is no law which says that other people must treat us fairly, or that it is a personal affront and an unforgivable outrage when other people are unfair. This is an irrational idea. If this should happen, it is best to focus on your own goal, taking into consideration some aspects of the other person's situation. How can you assert yourself in an unfair situation? Perhaps your self-respect would be increased by simply expressing your opinion. It is a waste of time to dwell upon the injustice of how you have been treated.

Discussion: Personal Rights

Discuss the following list of personal rights with the participants. As homework or a conclusion to this discussion, have participants record situations in which they did not act assertively. Ask them to consider the following rights. Which rights were involved? Allow participants to share and discuss this information.

❈❈❈❈❈❈❈❈❈❈❈❈❈❈❈❈❈❈❈❈❈❈❈❈❈❈❈❈❈

(📄 Workbook p. 20)

Personal Rights

- The right to refuse requests without having to feel guilty or selfish.
- The right to express my feelings, including anger — as long as I don't violate the rights of others, and to experience the consequences.
- The right to be competitive and to achieve.
- The right to have my needs be as important as the needs of other people.
- The right to decide which activities will fulfill my needs.
- The right to share my talents and successes openly without embarrassment.
- The right to make mistakes and be responsible for them.

Session 2

- The right to have my opinions given the same respect and consideration that other people's opinions are given.
- The right to change my mind.
- The right to be treated as a capable human adult and taken seriously.
- The right to be independent.
- The right to say "I don't know," and "I don't understand."
- The right to get what I pay for.
- The right to ask for information from professionals.
- The right to decide when to be assertive.
- The right to rest and leisure.
- Add your own: _____
- I am responsible for myself. I have the responsibility to recognize that everyone else has these same rights.

Think of a situation in which you did not act assertively. Write it down.

_____
_____
_____
_____
_____

What rights were involved?

_____
_____
_____
_____
_____

❋❋❋❋❋❋❋❋❋❋❋❋❋❋❋❋❋❋❋❋❋❋❋❋❋❋❋❋❋❋

Session 2

✳✳✳✳✳✳✳✳✳✳✳✳✳✳✳✳✳✳✳✳✳✳✳✳✳✳✳✳✳✳

(📄 Workbook p. 22)

Exercise: Others Rights

Think of another person or specific group of persons with whom you would like to be assertive or with whom you often have personal interaction (friends, patients, students, your parents, spouse, supervisor, coworker, children, etc.).

Write three rights this person or this group has in the spaces below.

1. _____

2. _____

3. _____

✳✳✳✳✳✳✳✳✳✳✳✳✳✳✳✳✳✳✳✳✳✳✳✳✳✳✳✳✳✳

Session 2

Exercise: Rights Auction*

(1 hour)

Purpose: To help participants learn to recognize that when one makes a decision to change, one gives up certain securities in order to obtain desired rights.

Materials: Enough pieces of 8-1/2" x 11" paper or cardboard for printing each right on a separate piece (plus extra blank sheets to use if two or more persons tie for a right); tape; marking pen.

Introduction: Discuss securities as follows:

> *In order to really accept rights for yourself, you must assume responsibility for your actions. Increased control over your life, greater self-respect, respect from others, and better interpersonal relationships are to be gained when you can do this. However, there are some risks involved as there are in every behavior change. You have received short-term benefits from being nonassertive including a way of behaving with someone you are familiar. You must be willing to give up some of these benefits or securities before you can act on your rights.*
>
> *Let's go over the list of securities in your Workbook (p. 23) and discuss each one in terms of its meaning to you as to short-term benefits and long-term expenses. For example, "I get protection from others," may be a short-term benefit you receive in return for letting others make your decisions. However, the long-term expenses include not being able to express your needs and having no control over your life. Is it worth it?*
>
> *Let's discuss the others. There may be some securities you are not ready to give up at this time — the risk feels too great. When you start feeling stronger, you may be better able to relinquish them.*

Procedure: Mount each card on the wall so that the participants can see the rights printed on them.

Ask the participants to focus on three or four rights they would like to own (ones they do not already own).

Have the participants remove the Securities for Rights Auction page (📄 Workbook p. 23) and cut or tear it apart on the dashed

---

*Adapted with permission from R. Egidio and S. Pope, *Becoming Assertive: A Trainer's Manual*, (East Lansing, Mich.: Michigan State University, 1976).

lines. Ask the participants to look over the securities and arrange them into three piles — one pile of securities they can give up fairly easily, a second pile consisting of securities that are somewhat harder to relinquish, and possibly a third pile that may be difficult or impossible to do without now.

✳✳✳✳✳✳✳✳✳✳✳✳✳✳✳✳✳✳✳✳✳✳✳✳✳✳✳

(📄 Workbook p. 23)

Rights Auction (Securities)
Are You Willing to Give These Up?

(Instructions: Cut along dashed lines.)

I get protection from others.	I avoid possible conflict/anger/rejection, pursuing only "safe" relationships.
I receive praise for conforming to others' expectations (i.e., I gain reward for pleasing others).	I believe the behavior of others is really responsible for my actions (i.e., others make me feel the way I do).
I must get my way.	I avoid the responsibility for initiating or carrying out plans (i.e., dependence on others).
I take the responsibility for others' feelings. (I will hurt their feelings and they won't like me.)	I maintain a familiar behavior pattern. It's too scary to try some other behavior, especially when I don't know how others will respond to me.
I protect myself from emotional involvement (i.e., I engage in superficial human relations to keep from being vulnerable).	I like being thought of as perfect (i.e., if I make mistakes, I'm no good).
I make hidden bargains instead of direct requests (i.e., putting up with obnoxious behavior in order to stay married or to get a promotion).	I have others make decisions for me. It's never my fault if I choose wrong.

Session 2

✻✻✻✻✻✻✻✻✻✻✻✻✻✻✻✻✻✻✻✻✻✻✻✻✻✻✻

Start the auction by asking: "Now, who wants to start the bidding? Which right do you wish to bid on? How many securities do you wish to bid and what are they? Continue the bidding by asking: "Who bids more for this right?" (All bidders do not have to give up identical securities. Each participant must tell aloud only the new security he or she is giving up. Help bidders realize what they are giving up by questioning them about the meanings the securities and the rights have for them.)

Give the posted right to the highest bidder to keep.

Discuss the securities the participants kept and the effect on their rights.

Suggestion: If there is a tie, give both participants the right. Have some "blanks" available on which to print duplicates.

Before the next session, participants should practice the rights won in the auction and record their reactions and others' reactions to the new behavior in their daily logs.

Exercise: Rights Role Play
(45 minutes)

Purpose: To allow participants to exercise the rights won in the auction as a first step in changing behavior prior to using these rights in reality.

Introduction: Since this may be the participants' first experience with role playing, you should model a role-playing situation. Choose a right that you would like to own (leaders are not perfect either!) and decide on the situation which gives you the most difficulty, such as economic transactions, work, or more intimate situations with your peers.

Choose someone from the group (or your co-leader if you have one) to role play the situation with you. Do not role play the situation perfectly assertively, but rather, how you usually do it. Ask the participants for feedback (positive and negative). Have them use the checklist (📄 Workbook p. 24) as a guide. If you are working with a co-leader, ask her or him for feedback, thus modeling appropriate responses.

With the benefit of the feedback, role play the situation again, this time assertively.

Procedure: Divide the participants into groups of three. Ask each participant to think of a low-threat situation in which they can practice the right they won at the auction.

Discuss the roles of the participants as follows:

Role of the Asserter: Asserter should briefly inform the respondent about the situation and the role the respondent is to play.

Asserters should not waste time talking about the situation, but should practice their behavior.

Role play should focus the message on what participants feel and/or what they want (e.g., "I feel irritated when I try to study with the stereo/TV going full blast.")

Role of the Respondent: Respondents should react naturally, as if they were the person in the situation.

If they feel defensive, guilty, or angry in response to the role player's attempts, they should act that way.

Role of the Observer: Using the Role Playing Rehearsal Observer's Checklist (Workbook, p. 24) as a guide, the Observer should check assertive behavior and write suggestions.

Session 2

✳✳✳✳✳✳✳✳✳✳✳✳✳✳✳✳✳✳✳✳✳✳✳✳✳✳✳✳✳

(📄 Workbook p. 24)

Rights Role Play
Role Playing Rehearsal (RPR) Observer's Checklist

Instructions: Check the assertive behavior demonstrated by the role player in the appropriate place. Write suggestions for improvement in the next column. Be sure suggestions are specific and refer to the behavior.

Assertive Behavior	RPR 1	Suggestions	RPR 2	Suggestions	RPR 3	Suggestions
Body language Direct eye contact						
Erect, confident posture						
No excessive or unrelated hand or body movement						
Content: Concise, to the point?						
Appropriately assertive to the situation						
Definite and firm						
Perhaps a factual reason but no long-winded explanations, excuses, or apologies.						
Stayed on the track						
How was it said? Almost immediately?						
No nervous joking or laughing						
No whining, pleading, or sarcasm						
Firm, unhesitant voice						

Session 2

Closing the Session

Before closing the session, assign and discuss the homework with participants. Close the session with The Link (p. 25).

Homework

Readings: 📖 Irrational Beliefs

Activities: ☑ Exercises in Concreteness
☑ Assertive Statements About Experiences
☑ Assertive Statements About Behavior
☑ Assertive Statements About Feelings
☑ Use the Rights Won in the Auction
☑ Make Three Positive Self-Statements to Others
☑ Daily Log

Homework Reading: Irrational Beliefs*

(📖 Workbook p. 25)

Albert Ellis and Robert A. Harper in *A New Guide to Rational Living* (North Hollywood: Wilshire Books, 1975) cite 10 irrational beliefs that are customarily learned and lead to distressful feelings. The 10 beliefs are numbered in a different order from Ellis and Harper. They are listed here according to how much general influence they have on people's behavior as suggested by Lange, Jakubowski, Ellis, and others.

The three most basic irrational ideas deal with the issues of personal rejection, personal competence, and fairness.

Irrational Idea

1

I must — yes, must — have sincere love and approval almost all the time from all the people I find significant.

Such thinking leads to never expressing opinions, avoiding conflict even when others violate personal rights, never expressing personal desires, holding back feelings (both positive and negative) and withdrawing from social interactions or intimate relationships even though desired.

2

I must prove myself thoroughly competent, adequate, and achieving, or I must at least have real competence or talent at something important.

This idea leads to the following responses: being extremely anxious to the point of being unwilling to deliver a presentation; worrying excessively over upcoming responsibility; prefacing every task with profuse criticism of external influences (not one's fault); avoiding social interactions for fear of having nothing worthwhile to say; avoiding trying out for enjoyable athletic events for fear of failure; being extremely anxious of expressing opinions as a new member.

3

I view life as awful, terrible, horrible, or catastrophic when things do not go the way I would like them to go.

Some people act on this irrational assumption by whining, complaining about, or bemoaning their "tragedy." Often they will withdraw into isolation or speak extremely bitterly about others (men, women, bosses, society) or act helpless and destroyed. They feel and act victimized.

Rational Alternatives

1

(A) I would like to be approved of by every significant person but I do not need such approval. (B) If I'm not approved of, I can try to determine what it is that person does not like about the way I behave and decide whether I want to change it. (C) If I decide that this rejection is not based on inappropriate behavior on my part, I can find others I enjoy being with. (D) I can determine what I want to do rather than adapting or reacting to what I think others want.

2

(A) I would like to be perfect or best at this task, but I do not need to be. (B) I'm still successful even if everything is not completely perfect. (C) What I do does not have to be perfect in order to be good. (D) I may be happier if I am successful, but success does not determine my worth as a person, unless I let it. (E) I will be happier if I try to achieve at a realistic level rather than a perfect level. (F) If I am not successful, I will likely be unhappy but not depressed or miserable. (G) It is impossible for anyone to be perfectly competent, achieving, etc. (H) Above all, if I demand that I be perfect, I will always be pushing or worrying when I slip. Instead, if I do what I want and what I enjoy as well as I can, I will feel happier and perform better.

3

This person has really treated me badly and I do not like the situation or that person's behavior. What can I do to change either? If I cannot change either, it is frustrating, but not dreadful and awful. I can begin to make plans for making my life as desirable and enjoyable as I can.

46

---

*Adapted with permission from A. J. Lange and P. Jakubowski, *Responsible Assertive Behavior*, (Champaign, Ill.: Research Press, 1976).

The next three irrational ideas pertain to aggressive blaming behaviors, nonassertive phobic responses, and denial of realities which do not yield perfect solutions.

Irrational Idea

4

People who harm me or commit misdeeds rate as generally bad, wicked, or villainous individuals and I should severely blame, damn, and punish them for their sins.

These persons usually behave aggressively. They may constantly criticize others for their incompetence, lack of sensitivity, ignorance, or evilness. Constantly questioning the motives of others or excessively berating persons who actually have been unfair is typical.

People not only use this irrational thinking on others, but also turn it on themselves. When they fail at a task, are rejected, or treat themselves unfairly, they then damn themselves for being wicked and often punish themselves

5

If something seems dangerous or fearsome, I must become terribly occupied with it and upset about it.

This leads to constant preoccupation with an unrealistic anxiety instead of thinking that could lead to control of the fearsome situation.

6

People and things should turn out better than they do and I have to view it as awful and horrible if I do not quickly find good solutions to life's hassles.

Many times people find themselves in circumstances where none of their options is desirable. When thinking irrationally, one bemoans that things should not be that way and that it is awful that they are, rather than accept reality.

Rational Alternatives

4

(A) I can tell people firmly and directly what they are doing that has negative consequences for me and I do not have to go as far as to punish them for their behaviors. (B) When I punish someone it costs me, too (in lack of energy). Seldom does it facilitate correction or change. (c) Just because I think something is wrong does not mean it is wrong. I (or others) may have behaved obnoxiously, unfairly, or incompetently, but that does not mean that I (or others) always will. (E) I can recognize and admit my own (or others') wrong acts and I can work hard to correct these misdeeds or their future occurrences.

5

(A) If I am not as good as I (or others) would like, I can handle it. (B) It is impossible to prevent a bad event from occurring by worrying about it; instead, I can think constructively and problem solve. (C) In all likelihood that event will not be as bad as I fear. Even if it is bad, I will not crumble. I can stand it even though it will be uncomfortable.

6

I do not need to overreact to these pressures. It does not appear that a "perfect" solution exists. I will accept that reality and do the best I can. I will determine my priorities and accomplish what I can in assertively communicating my limits to others. If others are not satisfied, that is unfortunate. I can work toward improving this situation.

The final irrational ideas represent four distinctly different beliefs. However, the behavioral results are all likely to be passive or avoidant. Persons holding these irrational beliefs also tend to take less responsibility for themselves and behavior.

Irrational Idea

7

Emotional misery comes from external pressures and I have little ability to control my feelings or rid myself of depression and hostility.

Some people believe that they simply "have a bad temper" or are "high strung" or are just always depressed. They have a genuine conviction that they can do little to change. Statements such as, "When things pile up, I just go to pieces," "He made me so angry," "I guess that's just the way I am," imply some external cause for their behavior and feelings.

Such people often hold the reciprocal belief that they can cause others to feel upset, angry, hurt, or miserable. Consequently, they hold back the expression of their opinions, feelings, or needs for fear of causing disturbance to others.

8

I will find it easier to avoid facing many of life's difficulties and self-responsibilities than to undertake more rewarding forms of self-discipline.

Some people "blow-up" if they do not immediately get relief from their irritations and worries. Nonassertive persons frequently believe that the immediate relief of discomfort is more important then the longer range displeasures resulting from avoidance and the discounting of their personal rights.

9

My past remains all-important and because something once strongly influenced my life, it has to keep determining my feelings and behavior today.

Such thinking supports passive behavioral patterns.

10

These persons learned ineffectual behaviors and believe they are necessary for survival. The behaviors may no longer be necessary for survival or a more effective behavior may now be an even better option.

I can achieve happiness by inertia and inaction or by passively and uncommitedly "enjoying myself."

A rationalization to cover fear of some activity. Such passivity breeds greater passivity to the point where an individual can become highly withdrawn and almost blunted to stimulation.

Rational Alternatives

7

Although one cannot make someone else angry or hurt, one can certainly behave in ways that make it very likely that others will respond with such feelings. We do not control others, but we can have some influence on them. Guidelines: (1) Determine how the other person is reacting to your behavior — is it appropriate and reasonable? (2) I can stand it when things go wrong; I can choose to stand it if I want to. (3) I have quite a bit of control over how I react to situations.

(A) If the person is hurt, angry, upset, or critical, check your own perception of your behavior. Did you violate the other person's rights? If so, admit it. If not, express regret at their response, but stand by what you said. (B) Others also have choices in how they react to me. I am responsible for my own behaviors and can accept the reasonable consequences. As long as I respect the rights of others. I do not have to take 100 percent of the responsibility for their reactions to me.

8

(A) Even though I get immediate relief when I avoid a disturbing situation or blow-up, I feel unfulfilled and that is often as frustrating. (B) What I am avoiding will probably not be as awful as I convince myself it is. (C) Avoidance does not ultimately lead to pleasure.

9

Although my past does exercise considerable influence, I am not fixed intellectually, emotionally, or behaviorally. I can change.

10

I can decide to involve myself with other people, in feelings, in creating things, or in ideas.

※ ※

Session 2

(📄 Workbook p. 28)

Homework Activity: Exercises in Concreteness*

In order to express your needs assertively to another person, you must be very explicit and concrete. Telling someone "I want you to respect me" is too general to be of much help to the other person. Telling yourself that your goal in assertiveness training is to be treated with respect is not much help either. It would be more helpful to decide what being treated with respect involves. For instance, it may mean "I do not want to listen to constant criticism."

Concreteness means speaking about *specific experiences* (what happens to me, what others do to me), *specific behaviors* (what I do), and *specific feelings* (feelings that accompany my experiences and my behavior).

Assertive Statements About Experiences

In the following exercise, you are asked to write about some experiences (what happens to me, what others do to me) assertively, first vaguely, then concretely.

Study the following examples:

Example 1: Vague statement of experience: "I want you to stop picking on me."

Concrete statement of experience: "When you call me 'Porky' or 'Tubby' I feel that you are ridiculing me for being fat."

Example 2: Vague statement of experience: "I'm not being treated right, I am being ignored."

Concrete statement of experience: "When you come home from work, you read the paper or watch TV. You don't tell me about your day and you are not interested in what I've done. Still if you feel like having sex you expect me to hop in bed with you."

In the spaces below, write about two instances of your own experiences. Stick to experiences as defined. Do not include feelings or behaviors. Express your experiences, negative or positive, in your own style.

1. Vague _____

   Concrete _____

   _____

---

*Adapted with permission from G. Egan, *Exercises in Helping Skills: A Training Manual to Accompany the Skilled Helper,* (Wadsworth Publishing Company, 1990). Reprinted by permission of Brooks/Cole Publishing Company, Monterey, CA 93940.

Session 2

2. Vague _____

   Concrete _____

   _____

Assertive Statements About Behavior

In the following exercise, you are asked to assertively write about some of your behaviors (what you do or fail to do) — first vaguely, then concretely.

Study the following examples:

Example 1: Vague statement of behavior: "I messed things up today."

Concrete statement of behavior: "I went away last weekend and didn't finish the report that was due today."

Example 2: Vague statement: "I carried off the interview and got the job."

Concrete statement: "I expressed myself clearly and enthusiastically during the job interview. I was able to show how my talents, knowledge, and experience would help their company and I got the job."

In the spaces below, write about two instances of your own behavior.

1. Vague _____

   _____

   Concrete _____

   _____

   _____

2. Vague _____

   _____

   Concrete _____

   _____

   _____

Assertive Statements About Feelings

In the following exercise you are asked to assertively write about some of your feelings (feelings related to behavior or experience), first vaguely, then concretely. Feelings should be related to the concrete experiences or behaviors that cause them.

Example 1: Feelings related to behavior (what I do).

Vague statement: "Thank you for inviting me, but I have a hard time at training groups."

Concrete statement: "I've decided not to attend that training group because I feel so embarrassed and hesitate whenever I try to explain what I mean."

Example 2: Feelings related to experience (what happens to me).

Vague statement: "My relationship with you bothers me sometimes."

Concrete statement: "I feel guilty and depressed whenever you call and say you are lonely."

In the spaces below, write about two instances of your own feelings. Relate these feelings either to your experiences or your behavior. Express them in your own style of speaking.

In the spaces below, write about two instances of your own behavior.

1. Vague _____

   Concrete _____

2. Vague _____

   Concrete _____

✸✸✸✸✸✸✸✸✸✸✸✸✸✸✸✸✸✸✸✸✸✸✸✸✸✸✸✸✸✸✸

Session 3
Blocks to Assertion

Overview

Goals: To reduce the anxiety participants experience in a specific situation; to increase the repertoire of effective responses for that situation; to teach participants how to recognize irrational assumptions and catastrophizing; and to teach participants how to replace these with rational assumptions and expectations.

Materials: Newsprint, marker

Contents: Homework Review
Exercise: Owning Rights
Mini-Lecture: Blocks to Assertion
Exercise: Relaxation to Relieve Stress
Exercises: Cognitive Restructuring
         Rational-Emotive Imagery
         Stop!
Closing the Session
Exercise: The Link
Homework:
- 📖 Reading: Dealing With Disapproval
- ☑ Activities: Developing Self-Statements for Coping With Anger
         Developing Self-Statements for Coping With Stress
         Practice in Cognitive Restructuring
         Daily Log

Session 3

Homework Review

Begin the session with a review and discussion of the homework assignment.

Exercise: Owning Rights (20 minutes)

Purpose: To develop participants' awareness of their rights.

Introduction: Discuss with the participants their success in "owning" their rights as practiced in the last session. Point out that success levels in owning the rights won in the previous session will vary. For instance, a participant may have recognized a situation as one where he or she should have assumed a right. This awareness should also be counted as a success. Another participant may have confronted an individual and have been very assertive on the basis of the right. There is a large range of success levels; all degrees of success are acceptable and are to be encouraged.

Procedure: Ask each participant to share his or her success in attempting to "own" the right won in the last session.

Notes:

Mini-Lecture: Blocks to Assertion

The following lecture defines blocks to assertion and introduces session goals.

Blocks to Assertion

What keeps us from being assertive? Most commonly, we use these four blocks:

✳✳✳✳✳✳✳✳✳✳✳✳✳✳✳✳✳✳✳✳✳✳✳✳✳✳✳✳✳✳

(📄 Workbook p. 31)

Blocks to Assertion

1. We do not believe we have the right — (socialization).

2. We do not want to take the responsibility for (speaking out, following through, our opinions, feelings) for fear of loss of approval, affection, hurting others, looking stupid, or being selfish.

3. We use irrational or mistaken ideas or assumptions.

4. We lack the skills.

✳✳✳✳✳✳✳✳✳✳✳✳✳✳✳✳✳✳✳✳✳✳✳✳✳✳✳✳✳✳

The blocks to assertion are interrelated. If we do not believe we have the right, we will not take the responsibility. Consequently, we may tell ourselves irrational or mistaken "self-talk" to rationalize our behavior so that we never have to practice assertive skills.

Many people are not assertive because of a belief system they have developed over the years. Sometimes their beliefs stem from childhood experiences at a time before they had developed the maturity to handle themselves adequately. Most of us are aware of the stereotypic behavior associated with the role we assume, whether it be that of woman, child, nurse, father, student, or teacher. Such stereotypes limit our actions and block assertive responses. Moreover, there are some situations in which most of us cannot realistically feel relaxed — for example, in a confrontation with a boss, or when speaking before large groups. The situation will vary with different people.

Our focus in this session will be on becoming aware of your thinking patterns, particularly those which lead to ineffectual behaviors. We will seek to change those thought processes to more productive ones (cognitive restructuring). More specifically, our goals are:

- To reduce the anxiety you experience in a specified situation.
- To increase the repertoire of effective responses for that situation.
- To teach you how to recognize irrational assumptions and catastrophizing and how to replace these with rational assumptions and expectations of how you will act in the situation and how other people might act.

Session 3

Exercise: Relaxation to Relieve Stress*
(5 minutes)

Purpose: To learn a way to relieve tension in times of stress.

Introduction: Tell three participants that learning how to relax is useful if you are nervous before speaking to groups, dealing with your boss, trying to get to sleep at night, or for many other reasons.

Procedure: Read the text which follows in a slow, relaxed, even voice.

Before we begin today, find a comfortable position. Move your body so you feel that if you let your legs, arms, or other muscles go completely limp, they would not fall, but would remain in a comfortable position. Now close your eyes and keep them closed throughout the session so you will not be distracted by light or anything around you. Although you may feel very close to doing so at times, do not fall asleep. Just listen to my instructions and follow them carefully.

The purpose of this session is to teach you how to relax and relieve all muscle tension. You will quickly learn the difference between tension and relaxation as I direct you to tense, hold, and then relax muscle groups throughout your body. You will also learn how to remove and replace tension with effortless relaxation. As each muscle group is relaxed, maintain its relaxation while you move on to the next group.

In this way you will arrive at a final state of deep and complete relaxation. As you become completely relaxed, you may experience pleasant and natural sensations of warmth and heaviness in your muscles.

Let's begin now. With both hands resting comfortable, make a tight fist with both hands and hold it. Tighter. Feel how the muscles pull on top of each hand, in the fingers, and in the upper and lower part of each forearm. Now relax. Let your hands and forearms drop and go completely limp. Remove the tension and replace it with effortless relaxation.

Now, while keeping both hands completely relaxed, tense the biceps muscles of both arms. Hold the tension and ob-

---
*With permission from Ruth Krueger, Western Michigan University, Kalamazoo, Mich.

serve how it feels as the muscles pull on top and under your arms. Now relax. Let the relaxation flow down your arms, both arms and hands becoming completely relaxed. Notice the difference between the tension and relaxation.

Now with your arms still completely relaxed, raise both your shoulders as high as you can. Feel the pull of the muscles across the shoulders as you raise them higher. Now relax and drop your shoulders. Allow them to sag lower and lower. Feel the relaxation spread from muscle to muscle.

Now squint your eyes tightly and wrinkle up your nose — tighter, tighter. Notice the tension building in your face and head. Now relax. Let all the muscles around your entire face and scalp completely relax. Experience the pleasure of calm, effortless relaxation.

Now tense your jaw muscles by biting your teeth together. Bite hard. Notice the feeling of tightness in your jaw muscles. Now relax. Let your jaws go completely limp. Let them sag and be comfortably relaxed.

Now push your head back as far as it will go. Hold it. Feel the tension in the back of your neck. Now relax. Return your head to its normal, comfortable position and relax.

Now take a deep breath. Fill your lungs full and hold your breath. Notice how the muscles pull across your chest, and how the tension builds. Now relax. Breathe out and breathe in normally, in and out. Notice how all the muscles of your body become more relaxed when you exhale. Go on breathing normally, easily, freely, completely relaxed.

Now making sure that your other muscles remain relaxed, tighten your stomach muscles. Make them hard and hold it. Feel the tension. Now relax. Focus on the surge of relief and the complete comfort or relaxation. Notice the general sense of well-being that comes with relaxing your stomach muscles. Continue relaxing, enjoying the calm, pleasant sensations of deep, total relaxation. Now arch your back — more — now relax.

Now I want you to tighten the muscles in the upper thigh portions of both legs. Feel the pressure as you tighten the top and bottom muscles of both legs. Now relax. Observe the difference between the feelings of tension and relaxation. Let your muscles go loose and heavy.

Session 3

Now I want you to tighten the calf muscles of both legs. Make them tighter. Notice how they almost hurt as they tense. Now relax. Notice the relief of relaxation as you let your muscles go.

Finally, push the toes of both feet hard into the soles of your shoes so that you arch up both feet. Feel the pressure in your feet. Now relax. Let your feet go and enjoy the calmness of effortless relaxation.

Now pay attention to your entire body. If you feel any tension anywhere, just remove it and replace it with deep, complete relaxation. You know how. Relax more and more.

[Long pause]

In a few moments I'm going to ask you to return to a normal state of waking tension. This does not mean that you will be as tense as when you came in, but just alert enough to go about the rest of the day's activities without any trouble. We'll do this gradually, so you won't be startled. I am going to count from four to one. When I count one, you will open your eyes and feel very refreshed and relaxed, much like you would feel if you had just awakened from a nice peaceful nap.

OK . . . four . . . three . . . two . . . (pause) one . . . Open your eyes. Stay as comfortable as possible.

Notes:

Session 3

Exercise: Rational-Emotive Imagery*
(30 minutes)

Purpose: To demonstrate the relationship between thinking and feeling; to demonstrate how feelings can be controlled by altering thinking.

Procedure: Read the following text to the participants:

Imagine an unpleasant experience or event you may have to face in the near future that causes you undue anxiety or anger. (Pause)

Close your eyes and think about the setting. Imagine the place where this event will take place. How does the other person look and behave? What do you say? What does the other person say? How do you feel when you start? Imagine when the other person speaks; when you speak. Don't try to avoid or suppress any of your feelings. Experience them fully, whether it is hostility, anger, anxiety, depression, embarrassment, or whatever.

Now start to force aside the strong negative emotions so that only mild disappointment or irritation is felt. Try to diminish your strong feelings.

When you have let yourself go through this procedure until you feel only disappointment or irritation, look at the thought process that produced these new, more appropriate feelings. What were the exact words? If you observe yourself clearly, you will find that you changed your belief system and consequently changed your emotions. Let yourself clearly see what you have done and what important changes in your thinking you have made. Become fully aware of the new beliefs.

List on newsprint some of the statements that helped diminish the negative emotions. Ask participants to discuss any that would also work for them.

Now fantasize the same situation you did before, only this time picture yourself acting in accordance with your new rational challenges. How did you feel this time?

---

*This procedure was first developed by M. C. Maultsby Jr., and Albert Ellis as described in *Techniques for Using Rational Emotive Imagery REI*, New York: Institute for Rational Living, 1974.

Session 3

Suggestion: In some cases, participants are unable to imagine themselves dealing with the situation assertively, but are able to picture someone else doing so. This can be an acceptable first step. However, the participants should be encouraged to eventually imagine themselves dealing with the situation in an assertive manner.

Suggest that the participants practice this technique systematically on a specific situation for 10 minutes each day.

Notes:

Exercise: Stop!
(15 minutes)

Purpose: To demonstrate the relationship between thinking and feeling; to demonstrate how feelings can be controlled by altering thinking.

Procedure: Divide the participants into pairs. Ask the participants to silently think about some disturbing experience or event they may have to face in the near future that causes undue anxiety or anger.

Suddenly shout "Stop." Ask the participants what happened to their thoughts. When the participants report that their thoughts went away, discuss how they can influence their thoughts. Ask them to state some realistic, rational self-affirming thoughts that they can use to substitute for a stream of negative thoughts. Have the participants tell their partners more realistic thoughts.

Say: "Now start your stream of negative thoughts. This time, you say "Stop!" out loud. Make your coping self-statements out loud, to your partner."

Ask the participants to start their negative thoughts again, but this time ask them to yell "Stop!" silently and repeat their coping thoughts internally.

Session 3

Discussion: Discuss how the "Stop!" technique worked in the group as a whole. Ask what happened to the participants' negative thoughts. Ask how their feelings changed.

Suggestion: Before ending the exercise, ask the participants to practice this technique at home for 10 minutes each night.

Notes:

Closing the Session

Discuss the homework assignment with the participants. Assign 10 minutes of additional daily practice on a specific situation with the Rational-Emotive Imagery and STOP! activities.

Close the session with the Link (p. 25).

Homework

Reading: 📖 Dealing With Disapproval

Activities: ☑ Rational-Emotive Imagery
☑ STOP!
☑ Developing Self-Statements for Coping With Anger
☑ Developing Self-Statements for Coping With Stress

Session 3

(Workbook p. 32)

Homework Reading: Dealing with Disapproval

You must be full of determination to change in the face of criticism from those who love you. Quite likely, as you become more assertive, you will encounter some criticism and disapproval from those who feel threatened by your new behavior. Those who have taken advantage of you in the past may object to your new assertiveness. If you never objected to being at their "beck and call," or catering to their wishes, they were relieved of taking responsibility for their own lives. Why shouldn't they object? Just remember, the reason for the protests and criticism is to force you to return to your former self, the self to which they have become accustomed.

If you can understand that others' complaints about your new behavior may be a strategy to divert you from becoming a different person, you will be able to ignore the criticism. Criticism which is ignored soon stops when it becomes obvious that such comments are ineffective.

Remember too that those who disapprove of your behavior are not thinking of you and your needs. They are only thinking of the inconveniences to themselves. However, you can reassure your family and friends that you are not rejecting them while you strive for some strength and independence. Let them know that after the initial adjustment, since you will be more contented, everyone may be happier and in greater harmony.

Acknowledge the fears of friends and family who complain with statements such as: "I suppose my new behavior is hard to understand, but it is very important to me to act this way" or, "I know that what I say or do is upsetting sometimes. I'm learning some new behaviors that are very important to me and it would be very helpful to me if you could tell me your reactions. However, I won't be pushed into becoming someone I'm not satisfied with" or, "If you want to talk about the change in me, I'd like to discuss with you how I feel and why this is important to me."

It may be difficult at times. However, keep in mind that it is an irrational assumption to expect anyone to understand you all of the time.

Session 3

(Workbook p. 33)

Homework Activity: Developing Self-Statements for Coping with Anger

Directions: Record self-statements you could use when dealing with anger.

A. Before the confrontation (preparation).
    (Example: "This is going to upset me, but I know how to deal with it.")

    1.
    2.
    3.
    4.

B. Reacting during the confrontation.
    (Example: "Stay calm. Just continue to relax.")

    1.
    2.
    3.
    4.

C. Coping when aroused.
    (Example: "Getting upset won't help.")

    1.
    2.
    3.
    4.

D. Reflecting on the experience. When conflict is unresolved.
    (Example: "Forget about it. Thinking about it only makes me upset.")

    1.
    2.

    When conflict is resolved or coping is successful.
    (Example: "I handled that one pretty well. It worked!")

    1.
    2.

Session 3

(Workbook p. 34)

Homework Activity: Developing Self-Statements for Coping with Stress

Directions: Record self-statements you could use when dealing with stress.

A. Preparing for a stressor.
   (Example: "What is it I have to do?")

   1.
   2.
   3.
   4.

B. Reacting during the stress-producing situation.
   (Example: "Once step at a time; I can deal with the situation.")

   1.
   2.
   3.
   4.

C. Coping with the feeling of being overwhelmed.
   (Example: "Keep the focus on the present; what is it I have to do?")

   1.
   2.
   3.
   4.

D. Reflecting on the experience.
   (Example: "It worked. I did it!")

   1.
   2.
   3.
   4.

Session 4
Refusing Requests

Overview

Goal: To learn and practice specific skills in giving and receiving compliments, refusing requests, resisting manipulation; to learn the value of persistence.

Materials: Newsprint, marking pen

Contents: Homework Review
Exercise: Giving Compliments
Exercise: Persistence – The Broken Record Technique
Exercise: Combining Persistence with Empathy
Closing the Session
Exercise: The Link
Homework
    📖 Reading: Saying "No" to Unfair Requests
    ☑ Activities: Practice Refusing Unreasonable Requests
                    Note Handling of Criticism and Compliments
                    Give Three Compliments
                    Daily Log

Session 4

Homework Review

Begin the session with a review and discussion of the homework assignment from the previous session.

Exercise: Giving Compliments
(30 minutes)

Purpose: To help participants learn how to give and receive compliments assertively; to demonstrate that positive interactions also involve assertiveness; to facilitate positive, supportive interactions in the group; to encourage participants to allow themselves to hear and receive compliments and to give them genuinely, thus increasing their sense of self-worth.

Introduction: Discuss the use of compliments as follows:

Many nonassertive and aggressive people have difficulty both giving and receiving compliments. Being assertive includes being able to express positive feelings and opinions also. Specific, enthusiastic feedback is helpful and builds confidence. Genuine compliments are important ingredients in any relationship — parent-child, husband-wife, friend-friend, employer-employee — because they maximize the positive elements of the relationship and increase the potential for rapport and better communication.

There are several ways not to respond to compliments. These responses would make it unlikely for the giver to offer another compliment. This is an example (Act out denying shyly, "Oh gosh, who me?") This implies that the compliment giver is wrong. What are some other examples of how not to respond to compliments? Let's act some out:

- *Returning the focus: "Oh, I like your skirt too."*
- *Put down: "Well, finally you said something good!"*
- *Rejecting: "You like this rag? I've have it for ages!"*
- *Egotistical: "Yeah, I'm really terrific!"*

There are also negative ways of giving a compliment.

- *Sarcastic: "Those pants really do fit well, don't they?"*

66

Session 4

- *Left-handed: "You finally cut your hair, it looks great now!"*

When we are young we are frequently told not to be conceited. There is a difference between healthy self-pride ("Thank you. I'm glad you liked my presentation; I prepared for it very carefully"), and egotism ("What did you expect? I always do well") which attempts to impress or "one-up" others.

Without healthy self-acknowledgment of your accomplishments, why should anyone else hire you for a job, let you take responsibility for any tasks, or like you if you do not like yourself?

Procedure: Ask the participants to stand in a circle. Ask alternate participants to give a genuine compliment to the person on the right. The compliment can be something the person has mentioned during the sessions that he or she is willing to be complimented on, or something else, such as appearance, sensitivity, manner, or sincerity.

Have the receiver respond to the compliment.

Suggest the following: "Try something like 'Thank you, that makes me feel good,' or 'I'm glad you like it, I like it too.'" Take a minute to think about what you will say and visualize yourself saying it.

Ask the two participants to interact briefly. Then have the receiver give a compliment to the person to his or her right.

After the compliments are completed, ask the participants to go around the circle again and briefly have each compliment giver express to the receiver something he or she specifically liked about how the receiver responded to the compliment. Make sure feedback is given directly to the participant.

Discussion: People vary in their levels of comfort when giving or receiving compliments. Participants might be encouraged to discuss their reactions during the exercise. If they seem particularly uncomfortable with either giving or receiving compliments, they should be encouraged to practice these skills in the future sessions.

Notes:

Session 4

Exercise: Persistence - The Broken Record Technique
Refusing Requests
(45 minutes)

Purpose: To teach the effect and value of persistence; to desensitize; to learn to recognize manipulation and develop techniques to counter it.

Introduction: Discuss the concept of persistence with the group as follows:

Nonassertive persons become easily frustrated and allow themselves to be manipulated by others into giving up their rights. Because of their frustration they back down at the first sign of what might be perceived as conflict. As a result, nonassertive persons teach others that they can be talked into anything. These are the people who are on the "can't say no" lists of organizations. These are the people who are asked to help all the time. It is helpful to recognize when you are being manipulated and be able to counter these efforts.

Manipulative people use these approaches:

Asking for reasons. "Why" questions trap you into long, involved explanations which can be countered.

Logic. This works if you have the same goal, but most people in conflict do not. The other person overwhelms you with the reasonableness of her or his requests.

Answers. You are made to feel that you should always have a ready answer. If you do not, then you must accede to the requests. (Do not forget about saying, "I need to think about that.")

Problems: The manipulator says, "We have a problem." Since many of us are trained to be helpful, we become involved in helping the other person solve his or her problem.

Understanding. It is expected that you should understand without being told.

Caring. You are told, "If you really cared or loved me you would."

You are told that you must never change your mind. (Remember your rights!)

Guilt. "I helped you before."

Changing the subject. "You want me to help tonight? That reminds me that John wants to know what we think about his report."

Helplessness. "I'm not any good at this. I've never done it before."

Remember:

- *You do not have to have reasons.*
- *You do not have to have answers.*
- *You do not have to have solutions to other persons' problems.*

Why do you use the Broken Record Technique to be persistent?

- *To make a request when the other person is extremely aggressive or manipulative.*
- *To refuse a request when the other person is discounting, manipulative, or destructive.*
- *To prevent someone from manipulating you.*
- *To settle a conflict on the real issues.*
- *To make sure the other person hears your opinion.*

How do you use the Broken Record Technique?

- *Keep saying what you want to say over and over again. Repeat your point in a matter-of-fact but firm way.*
- *Stick to your point. You can let the other person know that you understand his or her position, but you ignore side issues and personal attacks. Respond to legitimate points and perhaps give a brief explanation of your position.*
- *Keep repeating what you want until your request is met, or until your request is denied and all possible alternatives have been explored.*

Repeating your point, "ad nauseam," is only appropriate when the other person is extremely aggressive, destructive, manipulative, or discounting. For example, consider a situation where a father completely ignored everything his son said. Finally the son said in a voice loud enough to overshadow his father's, "I don't want to hear any more criti-

Session 4

cism! It hurts me!" This statement had to be repeated many times before the father stopped long enough to hear what his son wanted to say.

What if the other person is also assertive and is persistent?

Fine. Everyone should be assertive. You will settle differences between you by reaching a workable compromise, not by one person manipulating the other.

Caution: Don't forget that there may be situations in which it is not realistic to be assertive — the consequences may be too unpleasant or disastrous. These situations usually involve differences in power (such as between employer and worker). In these situations, you may want to accept compromises that you would not otherwise accept. On the other hand, you may want to be assertive despite the possible consequences. In such situations, each person has to decide whether or not being assertive is worth the risk (e.g., getting fired).

Procedure: Divide the participants into groups of three.

Start with the following commercial situation: saying "No" to a door-to-door salesperson who is selling insurance, encyclopedias, or pots and pans.

Instruct the participants to play their roles as follows:

Asserter. Responds only with "I understand, but I'm not interested."

Manipulator (sales person): Says things such as:

"What kind of person would do this?"

"No one else does it."

"What would happen if . . . ?"

"If you really cared . . . ?"

"Why don't you want it?"

Coach (helper): Comments on body language; keeps asserter to the point; helps manipulator with statements if necessary.

Have participants change groups and pick two persons with whom they have not worked. Ask them to role play a social situation, such as when a friend wants to borrow their car. Suggest that the asserter respond with "I understand your problem, but I feel anxious about lending my car," or disclose any accurate feelings. Perhaps a workable compromise will do — "I'll drive you where you have to go."

Session 4

                  Ask participants to change groups and choose two other people. Suggest a work situation, such as when a supervisor changes the participant's work schedule for the good of the company. Suggest that the asserter respond with an accurate feeling, for example, "I understand your problem, but I'm not too sure I feel comfortable with that. Can we work something out?"

Discussion: Discuss your reactions to the exercise with the entire group.

Notes:

Exercise: Combining Persistence with Empathy
(30 minutes)

Purpose: To show how persistence can be used to respond to legitimate points raised by the other person and may include an explanation of the asserter's position.

Introduction: Discuss persistence and empathy as follows:

        Social and family situations are often harder to handle than commercial or work situations. Usually a combination of empathy and persistence is effective. Remember that you are dealing with another person who has rights, problems, and feelings. Try to recognize these in your responses, be empathetic, and try to work things out if the requests are reasonable.

        The Broken Record Technique can sound uncaring and mechanical if used frequently. It may be better, especially with friends and family (those who are dear to you), to commu-

Session 4

nicate in your response that you have listened to what he or she has said and that you understand his or her position. Start with a statement demonstrating that you understand the other person's problems or feelings (empathy). See the chart in your ▤ Workbook, p. 35.

Next explain your position and note the differences between your position or opinion and theirs. Lastly, you say what you want done or what you're going to do yourself (action).

Session 4

(📖 Workbook p. 34)

Combining Persistence with Empathy

Step 1. Their position (Empathy)

Step 2. Your position (Explanation)

Step 3. Action (Your Message)

Example: "I can see how you really need the money . . . but I just don't have any to spare myself right now . . . so I've decided I can't lend you anything."

Example: "I realize you're in a spot . . . but I'm very busy myself right now . . . so I won't be able to do the work for you at this time."

Caution: Always try to respond to what the other person actually said by summarizing his or her statements. This will demonstrate that you are listening.

*If the other person is equally persistent, an assertive response is for you to negotiate a **workable compromise**. A compromise is assertive and workable if you are sure that afterward you will feel good about yourself and what you have done. In other words, you have said what you want. The other person has said he or she wants something different. To break the deadlock, one or the other of you suggests an **alternative** way of doing things that both of you can accept.*

The more alternatives you can suggest, the better chance you have of developing a compromise you can accept. Ask yourself, "How else can we solve this problem? What else could we do?" Ask the other person the same questions.

Procedure: Divide participants into groups of three and have them take turns acting as Asserter, Requester, and Coach.

Discuss the different roles to be played as follows:

Asserter: You may be helpful, but it is not your responsibility to solve the other person's problems. You are to repeat over and over again your basic message of refusal. Do not allow yourself to be manipulated. Remember how a manipulator operates. Do not forget — be emphatic. Try a workable compromise if the request is important or if you wish to practice doing so.

Session 4

Coach: You may help the Asserter keep to the basic message, and/or help the requester manipulate.

Requester: You may use any manipulation you can think of — guilt, logic, problem solving, etc.

Ask the Asserter to refuse a request such as collecting for charity, joining the PTA, or a friend asking him or her to babysit a dog or children.

Have the participants make new groups of three and role play a different situation. Suggest the following situations:

- Mother-daughter relationships
- A surviving parent striving to maintain control of his or her life
- A supervisor-employee situation
- A situation from a participant's own experience

Discussion: Discuss the participants' reactions to the role plays with the entire group.

Notes:

Session 4

Closing the Session

Before closing the session, review and discuss the homework assignments.

Close the session with The Link (p. 25).

Homework

Reading: 📖 Saying "No" to Unfair Requests and Demands

Activities: ☑ Practicing refusing unreasonable requests (record reactions in Daily Log)

☑ Note personal handling of criticism and compliments (record reactions in Daily Log)

☑ Give three compliments (record reactions in Daily Log)

✳✳✳✳✳✳✳✳✳✳✳✳✳✳✳✳✳✳✳✳✳✳✳✳✳✳✳✳✳

(📄 Workbook p. 35)

Homework Reading: Helpful Hints for Saying "No" to Unfair Requests and Demands

1. First, be sure where you stand (i.e., whether you want to say "yes" or "no"). If you are not sure, explain that you need time to think it over and will let the person know when you have an answer.

2. Ask for clarification if you do not fully understand what is being requested.

3. Be as brief as possible (i.e., give a legitimate reason for your refusal, but avoid long, elaborate explanations and justification). Such excuses may be used by the other person to argue you out of your "no."

4. Use the word "no" or "I've decided not to . . . " when declining. Both have more power and are less uncertain than "Well, I just don't think so."

5. Make your nonverbal gestures mirror your verbal message. Shake your head when saying "no." Often people unknowingly nod and smile when they are attempting to decline.

6. You may have to decline several times before the person hears you. It is not necessary to come up with a new explanation each time. Just repeat your "no" and your original reason. Remember persistence and The Broken Record Technique.

7. Use the words "I won't" or "I've decided not to," rather than "I can't" or "I shouldn't." This emphasizes that you have made a choice.

8. If the person persists even after you have repeated your "no" several times, use silence or change the topic.

9. You may want to acknowledge the other person's feelings about your refusal, "I know this will be a disappointment for you but I won't be able to."

10. Avoid feeling guilty. It is not up to you to solve others' problems or make them happy.

11. If you do not wish to agree to the person's original request, but still desire to help him or her, offer a compromise such as, "I will not be able to babysit the whole afternoon, but I can sit for two hours."

12. You may change your mind and say "no" to a request to which you originally agreed. That is your prerogative.

❋❋❋❋❋❋❋❋❋❋❋❋❋❋❋❋❋❋❋❋❋❋❋❋❋❋❋❋❋❋

Session 5
Expressing Feelings

Overview

Goals: To teach participants how to express opinions and needs; to demonstrate how assertion training improves interpersonal relationships.

Materials: Newsprint with the four fogging phrases (page 85), tape

Contents: Homework Review
Exercise: Admitting Mistakes
Exercise: Criticism (Negative Inquiry)
Exercise: Expressing Feelings Assertively ("I" Language)
Exercise: Desensitization to Criticism (Fogging)
Closing the Session
Exercise: The Link
Homework
 📖 Readings: Dealing with Criticism or Anger
       Negative Feedback to Others
       Disagreeing
 ☑ Activity: "I Want" List
       Daily Log

Session 5

Homework Review

Begin the session with a review and discussion of the homework assignment from the previous session.

Exercise: Admitting Mistakes
(15 minutes)

Purpose: To introduce and allow practice in admitting mistakes.

Introduction: Discuss admitting mistakes as follows:

When you have made a mistake, the assertive way to handle it is to admit it. Not only do you defuse the criticism by using negative assertion, but you also gain respect from the others by being honest and responsible. The conversation can then go to more constructive discussion about how to rectify the mistake.

Procedure: Divide the participants into groups of two. Have each person take a turn practicing the following situation (or use another experience of the participants' choosing).

A colleague has requested that a locked file be left out over the weekend so that it can be worked on. You forget. You respond, "I did it. I'm sorry, it was a mistake."

Have the participants continue the interchange until mutual satisfaction is reached.

Suggestion: Allow sufficient time following the exercise for group members to share and discuss their reactions to the activity as well as the implications for future behavior.

Notes:

Session 5

Exercise: Criticism (Negative Inquiry)
(20 minutes)

Purpose: To teach participants how to deal with criticism in a constructive manner without defensiveness; to resolve interpersonal problems and improve relationships.

Introduction: Discuss negative inquiry as follows:

Negative inquiry, or asking for specifics, allows you to change from dealing with vague generalized criticism to dealing with specific behavior. This in turn can lead to a decision to keep or change the behavior, or it can involve an assessment of the critic's perceptions.

Examples which could be shared:

Criticism: *"I don't like your attitude."*
Correct response: *"I don't understand. What is there about my attitude that you don't like?"*

Criticism: *"You are too aggressive!"*
Correct response: *"What is there about the aggression you don't like?"*

Criticism: *"You always contradict me."*
Correct response: *"What is there about the contradictions you don't like?"*

Criticism: *"You just don't seem to care about me anymore."*
Correct response: *"What do I do that makes you think I don't care anymore?"*

What would you respond to:

Criticism: *"You just don't deserve the raise."*
Correct response: *"I don't understand. What makes you think I don't deserve the raise? I thought I was doing a good job."*

Finally end with "Is there anything else I should know?"

Procedure: Divide the participants into groups of three. Have them take turns role playing the following situations:

- Wife says to husband, "You always watch television."
- Colleague says to worker, "You aren't doing your share."
- Parent to grown son or daughter, "You don't appreciate all I've done for you."

Session 5

- Employee to supervisor, "What do you think of my report?" (Supervisor has trouble criticizing, always wants to be agreeable. However, the employee needs constructive help before the report is submitted to the big boss.) In this situation, the asserter needs to first help the supervisor by saying something like "I'm not satisfied with this section, can you suggest anything?" and then "What about the next section? Is there anything else?"

Discuss the roles to be played as follows:

Criticizer: Uses one of the three statements and then responds to Asserter naturally.

Asserter: Responds with "I don't understand. What is there about watching television (doing my share, my not appreciating you), that you don't like?"

The Asserter should continue until specific behavior or values are disclosed, and the issue can be resolved.

Coach: Helps Asserter with phrasing and deciding when the situation is specific enough to begin to resolve the issue. The coach also should give feedback on assertive verbal and nonverbal behavior.

Suggestion: Avoid using "why" questions as this arouses defensiveness. Instead, try to ask "what" or "how" after an initial "I don't understand." Listen to humor. There may be hidden messages in quips or teasing remarks.

Notes:

Session 5

Exercise: Expressing Feelings Assertively ("I" Language Assertion)

(20 minutes)

Purpose: To introduce and allow practice in "I" language assertion.

Introduction: Discuss "I" language assertion as follows:

Assertion training emphasizes not blaming or ridiculing the other person. Helpful criticism focuses on a specific behavior rather than what the person is or is not. The four-step technique of "I" language assertion is a good model to follow, especially in expressing feelings, both positive and negative. It can also be used in asserting rights or for asking favors.

The four steps required for "I" language assertion are:

✻✻✻✻✻✻✻✻✻✻✻✻✻✻✻✻✻✻✻✻✻✻✻✻✻✻✻✻

(📄 Workbook p. 36)

"I" Language Assertion

Step 1. "I . . ."	You describe how the other person's behavior affects your behavior or feelings. If your behavior is not affected, you may be dealing with a difference in values. You still have the right to express your feelings, but will need to consider the other person's rights to her or his values.
Step 2. "When . . ."	You describe as factually as possible the specific behavior that either pleases or troubles you.
Step 3. "I feel . . ."	You describe your present feelings. Leave this part out if it is not appropriate to the situation.
Step 4. "I'd like . . ."	You describe what you want to do about the problem if it is appropriate to the situation.

✻✻✻✻✻✻✻✻✻✻✻✻✻✻✻✻✻✻✻✻✻✻✻✻✻✻✻✻

With "I" language assertion you take the responsibility for your own feelings instead of blaming the other person (I get angry v. you make me angry).

Example: It's damn embarrassing for me (Step 1) when wisecracks are made (Step 2) about me in front of other people. I'm madder than hell (Step 3) about being put down tonight. When you have complaints, "I'd like you (Step 4) to talk to me about them when we are alone.

Example: I have to borrow (Step 1) money myself to pay my bills when you don't make regular payments to me. (Step 2) I'm feeling more and more upset (Step 3) about this. I'd like you to at least start paying (Step 4) me something right away.

Example: I can get up (Step 1) in the morning and start my work without cleaning up a mess when you clean up (Step 2) after your party, son, without my having to remind you. I am really appreciative (Step 3) of your thoughtfulness.

You do not always use all four steps when using "I" language assertion. "I feel" may not be appropriate in employee-employer situations. Also, you might like to change the given order to suit your own speech patterns.

Example: When you're late (Step 2), like today, we have (Step 1) to wait for you before we can start and then we have to work harder to get a day's work done. I want you to be on time (Step 4) from now on. (There is no "I feel" statement.)

If you are criticizing a commercial service, complain privately to the person responsible soon after you notice the problem. Don't apologize. Be specific and try to compliment the person first, "Your food is usually wonderful and I enjoy coming here but I . . ." Criticize only those actions where change is possible.

To summarize, when you use "I" language assertion:

1. You talk about the person's specific behavior instead of attacking him or her.

2. You avoid the word "you" as much as possible.

3. You talk about the ways his or her behavior troubles you.

4. You take responsibility for your own feelings instead of blaming them on the other person.

5. You suggest the specific behavior you would like the other person to change about his or her behavior or suggest how the two of you might solve the problem.

Now we will try different ways of expressing ourselves first so that we can actually experience how using "you" as opposed to "I" affects us.

Procedure: Have the participants divide into pairs and take turns dealing with the situations below:

- Asking someone to quiet down.
- Telling someone that he or she did not do his or her share.
- Applying for a job advertised in the paper where the interviewer tells you that the firm is looking for someone with specialized experience which you do not have and which was not mentioned in the ad.
- You have received poorly-cooked food at a well-know restaurant.

Ask the participants to start statements with the word "you." Give the following example:

- When your roommate leaves his or her clothes all over the room and you say, "You're so messy! This place is a pig pen!"
- After the participants use "you" statements, ask them to practice the same situation using "I" language assertion.
- Have the participants discuss with each other how it felt to speak first from a "you" and then from an "I" perspective. Also have them discuss how it felt to be addressed in the two different ways.

Notes:

Session 5

Exercise: Desensitization to Criticism (Fogging*)
(15 minutes)

Purpose: To desensitize participants to criticism.

Introduction: Discuss criticism as follows:

Criticism is very difficult for most of us to handle. When you are tied up in knots, it is very difficult to focus on the matter at hand, much less to be assertive.

Fogging is not assertive behavior and has only limited value. It is a protective device which permits you to armor yourself while you decide how you wish to respond. It is also a technique to use with people who will not listen, who argue for the sake of arguing, or with whom you have tried to be assertive but have failed. Fogging is a way to protect yourself from the destructive criticism of people who imply that their values are better than yours; those who are not interested in hearing your side, only in wearing you down. Aside from our practice here for desensitization purposes, it is useful only as a last resort — to shut off further arguments.

This technique is called fogging because when using it, you act like a fog bank. No one can see through you, and a stone thrown at you will go right through — "ker-plop" — to the other side. It hits no resistance so that it cannot fall back to be picked up and used again. The other person's attacks have no effect and produce no results.

Practically every statement of criticism has some truth to it. Your response is to agree to whatever part is true. If it is true, (e.g., "you must be a women's libber! or "You made a mistake!") you respond with "That could be true."

If it is true in principle or logic (e.g., "If you stay out late every night, you'll get sick.") you respond with, "That could be true."

If the odds are that it might be true (e.g., Anybody who believes that must be a simpleminded half-wit.") you respond with, "That could be true."

If you cannot agree to any part of the criticism, you respond with, "I can see how you think that."

---
*Fogging concept developed by Manuel J. Smith, *When I Say No, I Feel Guilty*, (New York: The Dial Press, 1985).

Session 5

Procedure: Display the four phrases (📄 Workbook p. 37) somewhere in the room:

> "Yes, that's right."
> "Yes, that's probably true."
> "That could be true."
> "I can see how you think that."

Divide the participants into new groups of three. Have the participants act out the following roles:

- *Fogger:* responds to all criticism with any of the above statements and only the above.
- *Attacker:* criticizes everything about the Fogger's appearance (clothing, posture, facial expression, style of hair, manner of speaking, etc.)
- *Coach:* helps the Fogger respond with one of the four responses, then, as the Attacker runs out of criticism, switches to helping the Attacker think of barbs.

Bring the exercise to a close by saying to the group:

"You're not very good at this, are you?"

"You need lots more practice, don't you?"

"In fact, you are so bad, I had better make individual appointments with you so you can have lots more practice."

Ask the group to respond to each criticism with a fogging reply.

Notes:

Session 5

Closing the Session

Before closing the session, discuss the homework assignment with the participants.

Close the session with The Link (p. 25) exercise.

Homework

Readings: 📖 Dealing With Criticism or Anger
📖 Negative Feedback to Others
📖 Disagreeing

Activity: ☑ "I Want" List

✳✳✳✳✳✳✳✳✳✳✳✳✳✳✳✳✳✳✳✳✳✳✳✳✳✳✳✳✳

(📄 Workbook p. 38)

Homework Reading: Dealing with Criticism or Anger

Helpful Hints:

1. Relax and allow yourself to listen carefully to what the other person is saying. Breathing deeply may help you to relax.

2. Paraphrase the criticism so that the person knows you really heard and understood the point.

3. Ask for clarification if the criticism is vague or unclear, e.g., "You are rude." Ask for specific examples. (Negative Inquiry)

4. Decide whether criticism is fair or unfair. (Bring up your questions about the matter of fairness rather than the criticism itself.)

5. If it is fair criticism, ask for specific suggestions or alternatives such as what you might do to deal with the situation or behave differently.

6. Do not go into long, self-critical, or rationalizing excuses.

7. If you disagree, respond with an opinion statement using "I" rather than "you." For example, "I think my statement was misinterpreted," rather than "Your interpretation is wrong."

8. When responding to someone who is speaking loudly and at a fast pace, keep your voice lower and speak slowly.

Session 5

9. It can be helpful to share your feelings about the criticism. For example, "I'm annoyed that you're bringing it up again," or "It's not easy for me to take criticism."

Summary

When criticism is:	Technique to use is:
1. True	Admit the mistake directly.
2. Vague	Ask for specifics
3. Not true	Simple, direct denial

✽✽✽✽✽✽✽✽✽✽✽✽✽✽✽✽✽✽✽✽✽✽✽✽✽✽✽✽✽✽

✽✽✽✽✽✽✽✽✽✽✽✽✽✽✽✽✽✽✽✽✽✽✽✽✽✽✽✽✽✽

(Workbook p. 39)

Homework Reading: Negative Feedback to Others

Helpful Hints:

1. If you are bringing up an issue that has taken place some time ago, ask permission. Set aside a time and place, e.g., "I'd like to discuss something that has been bothering me. Do you have some time now?"

2. Be specific and give examples. Cite situations.

3. Use personal pronouns. Express your dissatisfaction without blaming, e.g., "It bothers me when you say . . ." or "I feel uncomfortable when . . ."

4. Avoid name calling.

5. Assume assertive body language. Be serious.

6. Give some suggestions, provide ideas, e.g., "I'd like you to call before coming over."

7. Give positive feedback as well as negative, e.g., "You really have been making an effort lately to do your share, but I noticed you didn't wash the kitchen floor this week as you planned. I'd like you to do it."

8. Do not let negative feelings pile up until you explode. Deal with them as they occur. Do not overload the person with criticism.

9. Avoid sidetracking. When people are uncomfortable giving and receiving criticism, they will avoid the issue by changing the subject or bringing up the past. Go back to the point.

Session 5

10. It can be helpful to express your feelings, e.g., "This is difficult for me to say, but I do want to talk to you about it."

✳✳✳✳✳✳✳✳✳✳✳✳✳✳✳✳✳✳✳✳✳✳✳✳✳✳✳✳✳

(Workbook p. 40)

Homework Reading: Disagreeing

Helpful Hints:

1. Acknowledge the other person's point of view, e.g., "I see your point, but I still think . . ." or "It sounds like this is important to you . . ."

2. Use an elaborated opinion statement to express your point of view, e.g., "I just can't accept your opinion because . . ."

3. Avoid name calling, e.g., "You're so pigheaded, rigid, dumb, etc."

4. Point out that this is an opinion, e.g., "I understand your opinion, but I still think . . ." "Often people forget that opinions are just that — opinions — and that they can change."

5. Take some time to collect your thoughts if you need to, e.g., "I want to think about that for a minute."

6. You have the right to your opinion without having to back it up with facts and figures, e.g., "According to what I've read . . ." or "I don't generally trust statistics, but my opinion is . . ." or "It is my belief that . . ."

7. If you can, share your previous experience with the other person, e.g., "I used to share your opinion, but my experience lately has been . . ."

✳✳✳✳✳✳✳✳✳✳✳✳✳✳✳✳✳✳✳✳✳✳✳✳✳✳✳✳✳

Session 5

✵✵✵✵✵✵✵✵✵✵✵✵✵✵✵✵✵✵✵✵✵✵✵✵✵✵✵✵✵

(📄 Workbook p. 41)

Homework Activity: "I Want" List

A. Make an "I want" list. Examples: "I want to be held when I feel sad." or "I want to eat out once a week," or "I want to be rewarded for the good work I do."

   1.

   2.

   3.

   4.

   5.

B. How realistic is each want?

C. For realistic wants, write under each the right that is involved. Write also the other person's right.

D. Now chose one "want" and write it below.

89

Session 5

How can it be achieved?

What do you say to the other person so that your wish is fulfilled?

E. Start to do the want you chose in item D and record the result in your log.

F. Go through the same process in order to fulfill any of your other wants.

✻✻✻✻✻✻✻✻✻✻✻✻✻✻✻✻✻✻✻✻✻✻✻✻✻✻✻

Session 6
Personal Situations

Overview

Goals: To integrate the learning procedures of the workshop; to provide carry-over to real-life situations.

Contents: Homework Review
Exercise: Breaking Into Conversations
Exercise: Behavior Rehearsal and Escalation
Exercise: Strength Bombardment
Exercise: Post-Session Self-Assessment
Homework:
  📖 Reading: Step-By-Step to Responsible Assertion
  ☑ Activity: Goal Setting
         Workshop Close

Session 6

Homework Review

Begin the session with a review and discussion of the homework assignments from the previous session.

Exercise: Breaking into Conversations
(25 minutes)

Purpose: To explore effective ways of breaking into conversations at parties or other social occasions.

Procedure: Divide the participants into groups of four or five persons and have them select one person in each group who has a problem with breaking into conversations.

Ask the other group members to stand close together and start a conversation on any topic — the weather, a trip, politics, etc.

Have the newcomer try to join the group and enter the conversation.

Suggest that the participants watch for the following points:

- Length of time before the newcomer spoke.
- Did the newcomer add to the conversation or bring things to a halt?
- Where did the newcomer position herself or himself?
- Was her or his statement a new topic? How did the others respond to it?

After a few seconds of conversation, ask the group members to give feedback to the newcomer on what was both effective and not aggressive.

Notes:

Session 6

Exercise: Behavior Rehearsal and Escalation
(60 minutes)

Purpose: To provide practice using situations of the participants' choosing; to integrate several already practiced procedures; to facilitate the transition from structured exercises to complex behavior.

Introduction: Have each person think of a situation in which he or she has difficulty acting assertively and complete the following in the workbook. It may be a situation from your "I want" homework.

❋❋❋❋❋❋❋❋❋❋❋❋❋❋❋❋❋❋❋❋❋❋❋❋❋

(Workbook p. 43)

Behavior Rehearsal and Escalation

Write a short, concise description of the situation:

_____
_____
_____

What is my objective? (describe in behavioral terms):

_____
_____
_____

What are my rights?

_____

What are the rights of the other person?

_____

What might be stopping me? Irrational thoughts? What are they? What can I say to replace them?

Self-Talk	**Rational Ideas**
_____	_____
_____	_____
_____	_____

93

Session 6

What techniques can I use to reduce my anxiety?

_____
_____

What do I want to say to:

Let the other person know I hear and understand him or her?

_____

Let the other person know how I feel?

_____

Tell him or her what I want?

_____

❋❋❋❋❋❋❋❋❋❋❋❋❋❋❋❋❋❋❋❋❋❋❋❋❋❋❋❋❋

Procedure: Explain the procedure to the participants as follows:

Move into small groups of four. Stand in a line. Each person in turn follows the steps below:

*1. The first person **briefly** describes the situation to his or her group of four.*

*2. The first person acts as the asserter and makes his or her assertive statement to the second person in line. The second person does **not** respond. (This first attempt is a try-out of the words and body language.)*

3. Using the assertion checklist (📄 Workbook p. 24), the group members give positive feedback, telling the asserter specifically what they thought was assertive about what and how he or she communicated.

4. The asserter is encouraged to determine if he or she agrees.

5. The asserter is asked what he or she would like to improve and the others are asked for one or two suggestions.

6. The first person, incorporating this feedback makes the original assertion to the third person in line.

7. The third person responds with a mild argument. The first person responds to the argument as assertively as possible.

8. The group gives feedback as above (#3 to #5).

9. Incorporating feedback, the first person makes a request of the fourth person who responds with a more severe argument.

10. The group gives feedback.

Notes:

Exercise: Post-Session Self-Assessment
(15 minutes)

Have the participants complete the Post-Session Self-Assessment (📄 Workbook p. 45).

Have participants compare results with their Pre-Session Self-assessment (📄 Workbook p. 4). Discuss significant changes.

Session 6

✼✼✼✼✼✼✼✼✼✼✼✼✼✼✼✼✼✼✼✼✼✼✼✼✼✼✼✼✼

(📄 Workbook p. 45)

Exercise: Post-Session Self-Assessment

Identify how comfortable you feel in each of the areas listed below. Fill in the blank spaces with an assertive skill not listed.

Assertive Skill	With Comfort	Need More Practice	Long Way Off
Saying "No"			
Asking for favors			
Making requests			
Expressing positive feelings			
Expressing negative feelings			
Giving compliments			
Receiving compliments			
Giving constructive criticism			
Receiving constructive criticism			
Meeting new people			
Initiating conversations			
Continuing conversations			
Talking about yourself			
Expressing opinions			
Refusing requests			
Asking for a raise			
Admitting mistakes			
Handling other people's anger			
Expressing needs			
Asking for information from authority figures (bosses, teachers, doctors, etc.)			

✼✼✼✼✼✼✼✼✼✼✼✼✼✼✼✼✼✼✼✼✼✼✼✼✼✼✼✼✼

Session 6

Closing the Session and Ending the Workshop

Review and discuss the final homework assignment on setting assertiveness goals. Also discuss post-workshop strategies for the participants, including:

1. Giving themselves rewards for achieving subgoals
2. Using resources for additional support when the workshop is over
   - Other members of the group
   - Friends
   - Family

End the session with the Strength Bombardment Exercise.

Exercise: Strength Bombardment
(15 minutes)

Purpose: To provide closure to the workshop; to allow the participants to leave with a positive experience.

Procedure: Appoint a participant to act as timekeeper.

Ask each member of the group to speak about himself or herself for one minute using only positive terms — no qualifiers, no criticisms, no "but's." Have the rest of the participants immediately give an additional two minutes of positive feedback to each of the participants.

Suggestions: The time allowed per participant may be varied to suit the group or individual needs. However, caution is urged. Do not allow enough time for painful and embarrassing silence. It is important that the experience be positive for each participant.

The leader needs to be prepared to fill any gaps in the feedback portion for the most "unlovable" participant, and to encourage the person who is too modest or a reluctant starter.

Notes:

Session 6

Homework

Reading: 📖 Step by Step to Responsible Assertion

Activity: ☑ Goal Setting

✳✳✳✳✳✳✳✳✳✳✳✳✳✳✳✳✳✳✳✳✳✳✳✳✳✳✳✳✳✳✳

Homework Reading: Step by Step to Responsible Assertion

This set of questions may be used to move step by step through the entire assertion process. However, you also have the option of selecting only those parts which are helpful at a particular time or in a specific situation.

1. Do I want to be assertive in this situation?
2. What is my objective? What exactly do I want to accomplish? (Focus on the issue in order to clarify the situation.)
3. What are my rights in this situation?
4. What are the rights of the other person?
5. What are some of the securities I get from my usual nonassertive behavior?
6. Why would I want to give them up in order to be assertive?
7. Am I stopping myself from being assertive by holding on to irrational beliefs? How can I replace them with rational ones?
8. Do I feel anxious about asserting myself? What techniques can I use to lower my anxiety?
9. What do I say to:
   - Let the other person know I hear and understand her or him?
   - Let the other person know how I feel?
   - Tell her or him what I want?
10. How can I evaluate my behavior? Did my nonverbal message agree with my verbal message? Did my assertion increase my self-esteem?

✳✳✳✳✳✳✳✳✳✳✳✳✳✳✳✳✳✳✳✳✳✳✳✳✳✳✳✳✳✳✳

Session 6

✳✳✳✳✳✳✳✳✳✳✳✳✳✳✳✳✳✳✳✳✳✳✳✳✳✳✳

(📄 Workbook p. 47)

Homework Activity: Goal Setting

Purpose: This last homework assignment will help you to set some goals for yourself so that you can continue to apply what you have learned in this *Assertion Training Workshop*.

Procedure: Think of an area you would like to improve.* Use guidelines as illustrated in the following example. Record that information in the space below ("Idea"). Next translate the idea into specific behavior. Decide on at least four situations where you can practice reaching your goal and arrange these into subgoals in order from least-threatening to most-threatening. Subgoal #1 should be attainable with only slight anxiety.

Example Idea: I'd like to feel better about myself.

Specific Behavioral Goal: I will consider requests and refuse them when I don't care to do what is asked.

Least-Threatening ⟶ **to** ⟶ **Most-Threatening**

| **Subgoal #1:** I will tell a solicitor at the door that I am not interested in what he or she is selling. | **Subgoal #2:** I will turn down a request from Susan to borrow my earrings. | **Subgoal #3:** I will refuse a date with John. | **Subgoal #4:** I will refuse to work overtime when I have a previous commitment. |

Idea:

_____

*Some guidelines to consider in setting your goal: Is it realistically attainable with the proper effort? Is it a reflection of your real feelings, rather than an expectation of others?

Session 6

**Specific
Behavioral
Goal:**

    Subgoal #1:

    Subgoal #2:

    Subgoal #3:

    Subgoal #4:

What reward can I give myself for achieving a subgoal:
1. _____
2. _____
3. _____
4. _____
If I need support, who will I call? _____

✸✸✸✸✸✸✸✸✸✸✸✸✸✸✸✸✸✸✸✸✸✸✸✸✸✸✸✸✸

Appendix A
Self-Assessment

Pre-Session/Post-Session

Identify how comfortable you feel in each of the areas listed below.

Assertive Skill	With Comfort	Need More Practice	Long Way Off
Saying "No"			
Asking for favors			
Making requests			
Expressing positive feelings			
Expressing negative feelings			
Giving compliments			
Receiving compliments			
Giving constructive criticism			
Receiving constructive criticism			
Meeting new people			
Initiating conversations			
Continuing conversations			
Talking about yourself			
Expressing opinions			
Refusing requests			
Asking for a raise			
Admitting mistakes			
Handling other people's anger			
Expressing need			
Asking for information from authority figures (boss, doctor, teachers)			

Appendix B
Daily Log of Assertive Behavior

Date	Behavior	Person	Satisfactory Aspects of Performance	Aspects of Performance that Need Improvement	Overall Evaluation (Excellent/Good/Fair/Poor) SUDS Score	My Behavior Appropriately: Non-aggressive Assertive

Appendix C
Screening Protocol for Assertion Training

OFFICE USE ONLY

We have a number of different levels of assertiveness training groups.

We would like to ask you a few questions so we can tell which assertiveness training group would be best for you. Also, groups are not always the best thing for everyone. If you are going through a personal crisis, such as divorce, this must be resolved first, before participating in an assertion training group.

1. Name _____

2. Telephone _____

3. Address _____

    _____ zip code

4. Have you been in any assertiveness training groups? ❑ yes   ❑ no

    If yes, of what duration? _____

5. What do you expect to learn from assertion training? _____

    _____

    _____

6. How did you hear about this group? Were you referred? By whom?

    _____

    _____

    _____

7. Do you think you need to become more assertive with: ❑ certain groups of people? ❑ in certain situations? ❑ to express feelings? ❑ in every area?

8. How do you see yourself in comparison to others? Are others: ❑ more assertive? ❑ less assertive? ❑ or about the same?

9. Does this person seem vague, extremely hesitant and passive, slow to understand? If yes, assign to Assertion Training 1A.

    Assign workshop accordingly.

1. *Introduction to Assertion Training.* One-day workshop — no previous contact.

2. *Assertion Training 1.* Six-session workshop — no previous contact.

3. *Assertion Training 2.* Six-session workshop prerequisite: Introduction to Assertion Training or Assertion Training 1.

4. *Assertion Training 1A.* For those referred by social mental health agencies, counselors, psychiatrists, hospitals, social worker psychologists. Also for those who seem extremely slow in thinking and/or speaking and who say they need help in every area.

Group

Date _____

Time _____

Leader _____

Place _____

Appendix D
Principles of Ethical Practice of Assertive Behavior Training*

I. **Definition of Assertive Behavior**

For purposes of these principles and the ethical framework expressed herein, we define assertive behavior as that complex of behaviors, emitted by a person in an interpersonal context, which express that person's feelings, attitudes, wishes, opinions, or rights directly, firmly, and honestly, while respecting the feelings, attitudes, wishes, opinions, and rights of the other person(s). Such behavior may include the expression of such emotions as anger, fear, caring, hope, joy, despair, indignance, or embarrassment, but in any event is expressed in a manner which does not violate the rights of others. Assertive behavior is differentiated from aggressive behavior which, while expressive of one persons's feelings, attitudes, wishes, opinions, or rights, does not respect those characteristics in others.

While this definition is intended to be comprehensive, it is recognized that any adequate definition of assertive behavior must consider several dimensions:

   A. **Intent:** behavior classified as assertive is not intended by its author to be hurtful of others.

   B. **Behavior:** behavior classified as assertive would be evaluated by an "objective observer" as itself honest, direct, expressive, and non-destructive of others.

   C. **Effects:** behavior classified as assertive has the effect upon the receiver of a direct and non-destructive message, by which a "reasonable person" would not be hurt.

   D. **Socio-cultural Context:** behavior classified as assertive is appropriate to the environment and culture in which it is exhibited, and may not be considered "assertive" in a different socio-cultural environment.

II. **Client Self-Determination**

These principles recognize and affirm the inherent dignity and the equal and inalienable rights of all members of the human family, as proclaimed in the "Universal Declaration of Human Rights" endorsed by the General Assembly of the United Nations.

Pursuant to the precepts of the Declaration, each client (trainee, patient) who seeks assertive behavior training shall be treated as a person of value, with all of the freedoms and rights expressed in the Declaration. No procedure shall be used

---

*Adapted and reprinted by permission from Assert 8, *The Newsletter of Assertive Behavior,* (San Luis Obispo, Calif.: Impact Publishers, 1976).

in the name of assertive behavior training which would violate those freedoms or rights.

Informed client self-determination shall guide all such interventions:

A. The client shall be fully informed in advance of all procedures to be used.

B. The client shall have the freedom to choose to participate or not at any point in the intervention.

C. The client who is institutionalized shall be similarly treated with respect and without coercion, insofar as possible within the institutional environment.

D. The client shall be provided with explicit definitions of assertiveness and assertive training.

E. The client shall be fully informed of the education, training, experience, or other qualifications of the assertive trainer(s).

F. The client shall be informed of the goals and potential outcomes of assertive training, including potentially high levels of anxiety, and possible negative reactions from others.

G. The client shall be fully informed of the responsibility of the assertion trainer(s) and the client(s).

H. The client shall be informed of the ethics and employment of confidentiality guidelines as they pertain to various assertive training settings (e.g., clinical *v.* non-clinical).

III. Qualifications of Facilitators

Assertive behavior training is essentially a therapeutic procedure, although frequently practiced in a variety of settings by professionals not otherwise engaged in rendering a "psychological" service. Persons in any professional role who engage in helping others to change their behavior, attitudes, and interpersonal relationships must understand human behavior at a level commensurate with the level of their interventions.

A. General Qualifications

We support the following minimum, general qualifications for facilitators at all levels of intervention (including "trainers in training" — pre-service or inservice — who are preparing for professional service in a recognized human services field, and who may be conducting assertive behavior training under supervision as part of a research project or practicum):

Appendix D

1. fundamental understanding of the principles of learning and behavior (equivalent to completion of a rigorous undergraduate-level course in learning theory);

2. fundamental understanding of anxiety and its effects upon behavior (equivalent to completion of a rigorous undergraduate-level course in abnormal psychology);

3. knowledge of the limitations, contraindications, and potential dangers of assertive behavior training; familiarity with theory and research in the area;

4. satisfactory evidence of competent performance as a facilitator, as observed by a qualified trainer, is strongly recommended for all professionals, particularly for those who do not possess a doctorate or an equivalent level of training. Such evidence would most ideally be supported by:

    a). participation in at least 10 hours of assertive behavior training as a client (trainee, patient); and

    b.) participation in at least 10 hours of assertive behavior training as a facilitator under supervision

B. Specific Qualifications

The following additional qualifications are considered to be the minimum expected for facilitators at the indicated levels of intervention:

1. **assertive behavior training,** including non-clinical workshops, groups, and individual client training aimed at teaching assertive skills to those persons who require only encouragement and specific skill training, and in whom no serious emotional deficiency or pathology is evident;

    a.) for trainers in programs conducted under the sponsorship of a recognized human services agency, school, governmental, or corporate entity, church, or community organization:

    (1) an advanced degree in a recognized field of human services (e.g., physician, counseling, social work, medicine, public health, nursing, education, human development, theology/divinity), including at least one term of field experience in a human services agency supervised by a qualified trainer, **or**

Appendix D

    (2) certification as a minister, public school teacher, social worker, physician, counselor, nurse, or clinical, counseling, educational, or school psychologist, or similar human services professional, as recognized by the state wherein employed or by the recognized state or national professional society in the indicated discipline, **or**

    (3) one year of paid counseling experience in a recognized human services agency, supervised by a qualified trainer, **or**

    (4) qualification under items B.2 or B.3.

b.) for trainers in programs including interventions at the level defined in this item (B.1), but without agency/organization sponsorship:

    (1) an advanced degree in a recognized field of human services (e.g., psychology, counseling, social work, medicine, public health, nursing, education, human development, theology/divinity), including at least one term of field experience in a human services agency supervised by a qualified trainer, **and**

    (2) certification as a minister, social worker, physician, counselor, nurse, or clinical, counseling, educational, or school psychologist, or similar human services professional, as recognized by the state wherein employed or by the recognized state or national professional society in the indicated discipline, **or**

    (3) qualification under items B.2 or B.3.

2. **assertive behavior therapy,** including clinical interventions designed to assist persons who are severely inhibited by anxiety, or who are significantly deficient in social skills, or who are controlled by aggression, or who evidence pathology, or for whom other therapeutic procedures are indicated:

    a.) for therapists in programs conducted under the sponsorship of a recognized human services agency, school, governmental or corporate entity, church, or community organization:

        (1) an advanced degree in a recognized field of human services (e.g., physician, counseling, social work, medicine, public health, nursing, education, human development, theology/divinity), including at least one term of field experience

in a human services agency supervised by a qualified trainer, **or**

- (2) certification as a minister, social worker, physician, counselor, nurse, or clinical, counseling, educational, or school psychologist, or similar human services professional, as recognized by the state wherein employed or by the recognized state or national professional society in the indicated discipline, **or**

- (3) qualification under items B.2 or B.3.

b.) for therapists employing interventions at the level defined in this item (B.3), but without agency/organization sponsorship:

- (1) an advanced degree in a recognized field of human services (e.g., physician, counseling, social work, medicine, public health, nursing, education, human development, theology/divinity), including at least one term of field experience in a human services agency supervised by a qualified trainer, **and**

- (2) certification as a minister, social worker, physician, counselor, nurse, or clinical, counseling, educational, or school psychologist, as recognized by the state wherein employed or by the recognized state or national professional society in the indicated discipline, **and**

- (3) at least one year of paid professional experience in a recognized human services agency, supervised by a qualified trainer, **and**

- (4) qualification under item B.3.

3. **training of trainers,** including preparation of other professionals to offer assertive behavior training/therapy to clients, in school, agency, organization, or individual settings

a.) a doctoral degree in a recognized field of human services (e.g., psychology, counseling, social work, medicine, public health, nursing, education, human development, theology/divinity), including at least one term of field experience in a human services agency supervised by a qualified trainer, **and** *b.)* certification as a minister, social worker, physician, counselor, nurse, or clinical, counseling, educational, or school psychologist, as recognized by the state wherein employed or by the recognized state or national professional society in the indicated discipline, **and**

c.) at least one year of paid professional experience in a recognized human services agency, supervised by a qualified trainer, **and**

d.) advanced study in assertive behavior training/therapy, including at least two of the following:

(1) at least 30 hours of facilitation with clients

(2) participation in at least two different workshops at professional meetings or professional training institutes

(3) contribution to the professional literature in the field

4. We recognize that counselors and psychologists are not certified by each state. In states wherein no such certification is provided, unless contrary to local statute, we acknowledge the legitimacy of professionals who are otherwise qualified under the provisions of items III.A and III.B and would be eligible for certification as a counselor or psychologists in another state.

5. We do not consider that participation in one or two workshops on assertive behavior, even though conducted by a professional with an advanced degree, is adequate qualification to offer assertive behavior training to others, **unless the additional qualifications** of items III.A and III.B are also met.

6. These qualifications are presented as **standards** for professional facilitators of assertive behavior. No "certification" or "qualifying" agency is hereby proposed. Rather, it is incumbent upon each professional to evaluate himself/herself as a trainer/therapist according to these standards, and to make explicit to clients the adequacy of his/her qualifications as a facilitator.

IV. Ethical Behavior of Facilitators

Since the encouragement and facilitation of assertive behavior is essentially a therapeutic procedure, the ethical standards most applicable to the practice of assertive behavior training are those of psychologists. We recognize that many persons who practice some form of assertive behavior training are not otherwise engaged in rendering a "psychological" service (i.e., teachers, personnel/training directors). To all we support the statement of "Ethical Standards for Psychologists" as adopted by the American Psychological Association as the standard of ethical behavior by which assertive behavior training shall be conducted.

We recognize that the methodology employed in assertive behavior training may include a wide range of procedures, some of which are of unproven value. It is the responsibility of facilitators to inform clients of any experimental procedures. Under no circumstances should the facilitator "guarantee" a specific outcome from an intervention.

V. Appropriateness of Assertive Behavior Training Interventions

Assertive behavior training, as any intervention oriented toward helping people change, may be applied under a wide range of conditions, yet its appropriateness must be evaluated in each individual case. The responsible selection of assertive behavior training for a particular intervention must include attention to at least the following dimensions:

A. **Client:** The personal characteristics of the client in question (age, sex, ethnicity, institutionalization, capacity for informed choice, physical and psychological functionality).

B. **Problem/Goals:** The purpose for which professional help has been sought or recommended (job skills, severe inhibition, anxiety reduction, overcome aggression).

C. **Facilitator:** The personal and professional qualifications of the facilitator in question (age, sex, ethnicity, skills, understanding, ethics — see also Principles III and IV above).

D. **Setting:** The characteristics of the setting in which the intervention is conducted (home, school, business, agency, clinic, hospital, prison). Is the client free to choose? Is the facilitator's effectiveness systematically evaluated?

E. **Time/Duration:** The duration of the intervention. Does the time involved represent a brief word of encouragement, a formal training workshop, an intensive and long-term therapeutic effort?

F. **Method:** The nature of the intervention. Is it "packaged" procedure or tailored to client needs? Is training based on sound principles of learning and behavior? Is there clear differentiation of aggressiveness, assertiveness, and other concepts? Are definitions, techniques, procedures, and purposes clarified? Is care taken to encourage small, successful steps and to minimize punishing consequences? Are any suggested "homework assignments" presented with adequate supervision, responsibility, and sensitivity to the effect upon significant others of the client's behavior-change efforts? Are clients informed that assertiveness "doesn't always work?"

G. **Outcome:** Are there follow-up procedures, either by self-report or other post-test procedures?

VI. Social Responsibility

Assertive behavior training shall be conducted within the law. Trainers and clients are encouraged to work assertively to change those laws which they consider need to be changed, and to modify the social system in ways they believe appropriate — in particular to extend the boundaries of human rights. Toward these ends, trainers are encouraged to facilitate responsible change skills *via* assertive behavior training. All those who practice, teach, or do research on assertive behavior are urged to advocate caution and ethical responsibility in application of the technique, in accordance with these Principles.

Appendix E
Suggested Agenda for a One-Day Workshop

- 9:00   Complete Assertive Self-Assessment
- 9:15   Learning to distinguish differences among aggressive, assertive, and nonassertive behavior
- 10:00   Blocks to assertion:
  - Personal Rights
  - Irrational Beliefs
- 11:00   Identifying personal pattern of blocks to assertion
- 11:45   Skill: Fogging (desensitization to criticism)
- 12:00   Lunch
- 1:00   Skill: Learning voice level and force ("No, I won't." — "Yes, you will.")
- 1:20   Counteracting Irrational Beliefs
- 2:00   Skills:
  - Indirect *v.* Direct Requests
  - "I" Statements
  - Body Language
- 2:30   Behavior Rehearsal and Escalation Exercise
- 3:00   Summary
- 3:15   Evaluation and Closure
- 3:30   Dismissal

Appendix F
Advanced Assertion Training
(For General Populations)

Suggested Agenda for a Six-Session Workshop

Session 1 Self-Assessment
Review Definitions
Review Rights
Review Irrational Beliefs
Expressing Liking, Loving, and Affection

Session 2 Initiating or Maintaining Conversations
Refusing Dates and/or Social Engagements

Session 3 Speaking Before Groups — Public Speaking
Practicing Stress Reduction — Relaxation

Session 4 Handling Anger — Withdrawal
Yours
Others

Session 5 Being Assertive with Authority Figures
Professionals
Bosses
Teachers

Session 6 Being Assertive with Parents and Family Members
Self-Assessment
Closure

Appendix G
Glossary*

Aggressive behavior. Standing up for one's rights and expressing one's thoughts, feelings, and beliefs in a way that is dishonest, usually inappropriate, and violates the rights of the other person. The goal is domination or winning by humiliating, degrading, belittling, insulting, or overpowering another person.

Assertive behavior. Being able to express one's feeling, make free choices and meet more of one's personal needs without experiencing undue guilt or anxiety and without violating the rights and dignity of others.

Behavior rehearsals. Role play usually combined with other techniques such as modeling, covert rehearsal, and positive reinforcement.

Broken record — persistence. A technique in which one repeats what one wants over and over again without getting angry, loud, or irritated. Can be used with manipulative, aggressive persons so as to be heard and to keep from being drawn into side issues.

Cognitive-restructuring, rational-emotive procedures. Methods for teaching persons how to become aware of their thought patterns and to develop more rational ways of thinking. Changes in thinking will help alter undesirable behaviors in a particular situation.

Covert rehearsal. The process of imagining oneself responding successfully, or as one would like to, in a particular problem situation.

Feedback. Any kind of return information from a source which is useful in regulating behavior.

Fogging. A nondefensive technique to desensitize oneself to manipulative criticism in which one puts psychological distance between oneself and the criticizer. It is a passive rather than an assertive skill and should only be used as a last resort, to shut off further arguments.

Generally nonassertive. Being nonassertive in most situations and with most people.

Negative assertion. Admitting mistakes honestly and forthrightly.

Negative inquiry. Asking for specifics in a vague or general criticism.

Nonassertive-aggressive (NAG). Failing to stand up for yourself initially, then sabotaging the situation later so that the other person feels humiliated, guilty, punished, or angry.

---
*The Glossary is also listed on page 49 of the *Participant Workbook*.

Appendix G

Nonassertive behavior. (1) Violating your rights by either failing to express your honest feelings, thoughts, and beliefs, and consequently permitting others to take advantage of you, or (2) expressing your thoughts, beliefs, and feelings in such an apologetic, cautious, and unconfident manner that other people can disregard them.

Modeling. Demonstrating for an observer a behavior the observer wishes to learn.

Role play. Acting out or replicating a situation in which one plays a role or practices behavior that one would like to use in a similar, real-life situation.

Self-assertion. A self-measurement instrument to assess assertive behavior before and after training. The instrument provides information on the areas in which trainees may want to improve their skills and the progress they have made.

Situationally nonassertive. Behaving nonassertively in certain situations or with certain people but being able to be assertive otherwise.

Self-concept, self-esteem. The individual's evaluation of himself or herself.

Self-disclosure. Behavior which reveals the self.

Significant others. Persons in the immediate environment who exert psychological influence on the individual.

SUDs Score (Subjective Unit of Disturbance). A scale of zero to 100 measuring one's subjective level of anxiety.

Thought stoppage. The technique of controlling unwanted thoughts through negative self-reinforcement, specifically by using the word "stop" at first shouted aloud and eventually said silently to oneself.

Workable compromise. An alternate way of doing things that both parties accept. Negotiating an acceptable solution.

Appendix H
What Do You Say?

Some Typical Problems Arising in Assertion Training Workshops

- What do you say to the participant who asks, "must I be assertive?"

    You are always free to choose not to assert yourself; assuming you are willing to take the responsibility for whatever consequences may occur. The issue or relationship may not be important to you, you may not wish to take the time or there may be too much to at risk. The important thing is that you make the choice so that you feel in control. You need to ask yourself, how will I feel afterwards if I don't assert myself in this situation? However, if you find yourself deciding to be nonassertive most of the time, you will need to question your decision.

- Participant who says something like I've always done it this other way and it works fine, **or** I don't need to tell them I'm angry, they know.

    That's fine. We certainly are not looking for problems if there are none. However, you may want to try your usual response with the other members of your triad and then try ours. Get feedback from them on how they react. Then decide which seems better to you.

- Group who has gotten off the track and is gossiping or just visiting with each other.

    Whose turn is it to practice . . . ?

- Person who is avoiding roleplaying by endlessly describing the situation.

    What is it you would like to say to that person? Try it on your partner.

- Person who takes up too much of your time asking endless questions or telling endless anecdotes.

    Thank you for your contribution (question) but I need to move on (or find out what the others think).

- Person whose inappropriate, sometimes, bizarre remarks, questions, and actions are making the other members uncomfortable. It is obvious this person has some emotional problems or is perhaps going through an emotional crisis.

    Assertive groups don't benefit everyone. I would be glad to refer you to a group that would fit your needs better or to a person who could help you on a one-to-one basis. (This should be said to the participant in private.)

Appendix H

- The person who says, "Our church teaches us to turn the other cheek."

    The Scriptures also say, "Love thy neighbor as thyself." You pay for the same sort of service as a nonChristian does. You deserve the same sort of respect. Christ was assertive when He threw the money changers out of the temple. In Act 16:35-40, Paul had been thrown into prison and when the authorities discovered he was a Roman citizen being held without trial, they attempted to release him without a fuss. But Paul demanded the same treatment any other Roman would have received. He demanded they come and let him out personally.

    Also, when you refuse to permit the other person to know your relevant feelings, opinions, or desires you are judging that person incapable of handling them.

- Person with internal conflicts about being assertive.

    Try the empty chair technique. Have the person talk to her or his assertive self, describing feelings and conflicts. Then have the person switch chairs allowing his or her assertive self to answer. Do this until the problem seems clarified.

Appendix I
Bibliography

Adams, Linda, and Elinor Lenz. *Effectiveness Training for Women.* New York: Berkley Publishing Group, 1989.

Alberti, Robert (ed.). *Assertiveness Innovations, Applications, Issues.* San Luis Obispo: Impact Publishers, 1977.

Alberti, Robert E., and Michael L. Emmons. *Your Perfect Right.* Impact Publishers, San Luis Obispo: Impact Publishers, 1995.

Arling, Charles E. *Holy Boldness.* Chappaqua, N.Y.: Christian Herald Books, 1980.

Bloom, Lynn Z., Karen Coburn, and Loan Perlman. *The New Assertive Woman.* New York: Dell Books, 1976.

Bower, S. A. *Asserting Yourself.* San Francisco: Addison Wesley Longman, 1991.

The Counseling Psychologist. *Assertion Training* 5, no. 4 (1975).

Egan, Gerald. *The Skilled Helper: Exercise in Helping Skills.* Monterey, Calif.: Brooks, Cole, 1990.

Egidio, R., and S. Pope. *Becoming Assertive: A Trainer's Manual.* East Lansing, Mich.: Michigan State University, 1976.

Ellis, Albert, and R. A. Harper. *A New Guide to Rational Living.* Englewood Cliffs, N.J.: Prentice-Hall, 1978.

Fensterheim, H., and J. Baer. *Don't Say Yes When You Want to Say No.* New York: Dell, 1975.

Galassi, Merna Dee, and John P. Galassi. *Assert Yourself: How to Be Your Own Person.* New York: Human Sciences Press, 1977.

Gordon, Thomas. *Parent-Effectiveness Training.* New York: Peter H. Wyden, 1974.

Jakubowski, Patricia. "Facilitating the Growth of Women Through Assertion Training," *Counseling Psychologists* 4, no. 1 (1973).

Kirchner, E. P., and R. E. Kennedy. *Leaders Manual for an Assertive Skills Course in Correctional Settings.* Institute for Research on Human Resources, University Park, Penn.: Pennsylvania State University, 1978.

Kirschner, R., and R. Brinkman. *Dealing with People You Can't Stand.* New York: McGraw-Hill, 1994.

Lange, Arthur J., and Patricia Jakubowski. *Responsible Assertive Behavior.* Champaign, Ill.: Research Press, 1976.

Lazurus, Arnold, and Allen Fay. *I Can If I Want To.* New York: William Morrow and Company, 1992.

Maultsby, M. C. Jr., and A. Ellis. *Technique for Using Rational-Emotive Imagery (REI).* New York: Institute for Rational Living, 1974.

McNerlage, Linda A., and Kathleen A. Adams. *Assertiveness at Work.* Englewood Cliffs, N.J.: Prentice-Hall, 1982.

Phelps, S., and Nancy Austin. *The Assertive Woman: A New Look.* San Luis Obispo: Impact, 1987.

Smith, Manuel J. *When I Say No, I Feel Guilty.* New York: Bantam Books, 1975.

Wolpe, J. *The Practice of Behavior Therapy,* 2nd. ed. New York: Pergamon Press, 1982.